ESKIMO DIARY

Thomas Frederiksen

ESKIMO DIARY

Foreword by Emil Rosing
English translation by Jack Jensen and Val Clery
Caligraphy by Mel Poteck

NELSON · CANADA

Published in Canada by Nelson Canada Limited, 1980

© Thomas Frederiksen 1980
ISBN 0-17-601445-4

Printed and bound in Portugal by Trama/Plurigraf 1980

An international co-production

arranged by Gyldendal, Copenhagen

Foreword

Thomas Frederiksen was born in Igíniarfik in 1939. His forefathers on both sides were famed in their district as great hunters. At that time, the whole basis of life was hunting, which was governed by various unwritten laws. Hunters alternated between hunting districts in order not to over-hunt in any one place.

Thomas and his brothers were brought up as hunters and have always been involved in fishing. Today, techniques and modern civilisation have become such decisive factors in daily life that the risk of over-hunting has increased, because, among other things, the importance of distance has lessened. And in Greenland we see over and over again how human influence on nature disturbs its rhythm.

In the old days, Greenland society was static and no great changes in culture or trade occurred. Experience was passed from generation to generation through accounts and stories of everyday life, cultural life being reinforced as a result. The art of story-telling was enriching and educational, giving colour to everyday life.

Art was very much a part of daily life; the decoration of household articles and hunting equipment, the carving of sculptures, patterns in clothing and the decorations of the women's leatherwork all added pleasure to everyday living.

Since early youth, Thomas has kept a diary for his own amusement, noting down events and experiences of his own as well as those told him by others. He appreciates Greenland humour and delights in the use of genuine Greenland expressions. Sometimes he shows his pride of and respect for his forefathers by reviving tales and legends, at the same time, describing developments and their consequences. He considers it important to be concerned with future development so that it is guided to the benefit of the community.

Two years ago, I discovered that Thomas had handed his diary to *Grafisk Vaerksted* (Graphic Workshop) in Godthåb (Nûk) with the remark: 'Hope you will enjoy it and find inspiration and pleasure from it.'

The contents are a small social and cultural history in pictures and text. Like his forefathers, Thomas has drawn his greatest inspiration from the sea.

My thanks to Thomas for his co-operation in making his diary available to a great many people.

March 1980
Emil Rosing

6

Kânâk

Upernavik

Ûmának

Kemertarssuaк
Ausiait

Kulissat
Kasigiánguit

Iqdlorнarlut

Sisimiut

Manîtsoк

Angmagssalik

Nûk

Pâmiut

Ivigtût
Nareortoк

My First Illustration In Colour

When I was only 15 years old, this is how it used to look whenever a hunter came back from the hunt in the Northlands.

It was always exciting when my father brought home a seal. My mother would skin it and would share the meat with everybody in our hamlet.

Sharing the catch from the hunt is a local tradition, and it always made us happy to see the pleasure of neighbours, especially those who were poor and had children, when they got their share.

8

umingara siyugdlee

15.-ni nik ukiorcardluga amirpara tássa kimugsere A
vangnámiok likítoe   pisarnerput na-
yorkuteraluga. ila miánertawaok atáta pisarkwermae.
lluve likíkága me.

nexálo aránag pu-
lagtaryiá, nunarivatimitello pajugdluere miánu-
taeaoe, scaleingmik pûgssåleeireut. nûweatdlo
miánármerat miánwajúmúngtairnu ayamag
tairput miániardlugit pisava tocaráganile i mi tae
malut pajugterlarput. ie ujanartaeritollo

Thomas Frederiksen

This is another memory from about the same time. It shows a great lake in the North, where I have only been once, but where our people have always gone to camp and hunt reindeer as long as anyone can remember.

As the picture shows, the hunters have just brought in a reindeer buck. It is said that in those days, anyone, man or woman, was strong enough to carry a whole reindeer.

"äma äuna 15 ininte ukionardlunga ássuliāiaróra, Nágsugtūq, saserssuane āvaial alángerne temärsimärtut sarkáne kangrane ină dássagör kāra Angtorarajugtor.

            saima äma sakordluqáinarmik a mingaróra dekuiksiarsimasara najorreutaraluga.

     vēnata pangmarssuae likernsimavā ilugtūsitzdlugo saima sujuliqut nakūisimatigās ilāningōr äma ernat pangnerit ilüngaisa, sikeúitarpait nangmagdlugit.

Thomas Frederiksen

This is an imaginary scene I painted many years ago. It shows kayaks and a skin-covered women's boat during a whale hunt. Traditionally, only men took part in the whale hunt, but in some places in the old days women, dressed in their parkas, were used to row the boats.

Special names are given to each stage of the whale hunt. This shows a whale being harpooned at the Anguvigartorfik, or Place of Harpooning. Seal bladders are attached to the harpoon to prevent the whale from escaping. When a whale does escape and goes aground, that is called the Altu, or The Touching. And wherever the whale is finally killed is called the Arfiorfik, or The Whale Hunt Place.

3.

uma tássa áakordlúngarnar 1933-me amingara
arfangmiat umiat kaïnatdlo angutaimarssu-
nôr arfangmiartaranuk? (Sanmiamik umat tugtut
umínik atisar tássa Anguvingarfiup avatâne arfer
kaïnap umiatdlo sujugtuata avatartaluât atg-
to agtormago ãma atsingssimavât Avignier-
miap avatâne Ôtagfingme pisarsimavât.
        Arfersiorfingmuk malirssulivamig-
ko (tauvane ãma kalirtalivarfiipavamakarpia)
        Atartussoer Thomas Frederiksen
                Igminiarfin.

This picture shows a group of walruses afloat on an ice pack along the Western shore. In the old days, when walruses were plentiful, this was a very common sight.

Here, with the sun sinking in the West, a group of walruses aboard their icy boat float in towards the shore.

14

àᵗƒiꝗ ꝛaꞋꞋimassut ᵗáᵘꞋná ⁴ ǟma (ꞋAꞋꝛordlŏꝛdlⁱⁿgo ᵉ
summᵘmerꝗᵒ˟ ꝛanga aᵒᵗƒⁱᵗ ᵗⁱⁱᵛfarⁱmaꞋarat ᵈllaꞋ
mǟla sᵘᵘnᵘᵘ lⁱⁱᵗⁱᵐᵘᵗ taⁱrilⁱᵗˢᵒⁿ pⁱᵗⁱˊᵛaᵗᵘ.
namt taliⁱtⁱᵗˢᵒⁿ (ⁱmawa ᵗⁱᵗˢarˢⁱˣp ᵗⁱarrᵒⁱᵗᵘ
ⁿgäᵗⁱᵉˊ) Tⁱⁱᵈᵘᵐⁱⁱᵗᵘᵗⁱᵗ ᵗⁱᵗⁱᵗˢᵗⁱᵗⁱˣ auᵗⁱᵗⁱᵗⁱᵗⁱᵗⁱᵗⁱᵗⁱᵗⁱ ᵗⁱᵗⁱᵗˢᵘᵗⁱᵗⁱᵗ ᵗra
lⁱ˟ᵈlⁱⁱᵗ   J.ꞋMⁱᵗᵗⁱˣ
ⁱ̇ ⁱmⁱᵗ tauwaⁿⁱ ⁱⁱᵗⁱᵗ˟ⁱᵗⁱᵗⁱᵗⁱᵗⁱⁱmaᵍᵃⁱᵗⁱ ⁱᵗⁱᵗ˟ᵗⁱ
ᵗⁱᵗ avaⁱᵗⁱᵗ ⁱᵗⁱˊ ⁱᵗˊᵘᵍⁱᵗⁱⁱᵗⁱᵗⁱⁱⁱᵗ ⁱ̇ᵗⁱᵗⁱᵗⁱᵗⁱᵗⁱᵍⁱlⁱᵗⁱⁱⁱ ⁱ
lⁱⁱᵗ ⁱᵗⁱᵗˊⁱᵗⁱ˟ⁱᵗ ⁱᵗᵗⁱᵗⁱᵗⁱᵗ˟ⁱᵗⁱⁱⁱᵗⁱ ⁱᵗⁱᵗˊⁱⁱᵗⁱ˟ⁱᵗ ⁱᵗⁱᵗⁱᵗⁱⁱᵗⁱᵗ
ⁱᵗⁱᵗⁱⁱⁱᵗⁱ ⁱlⁱⁱᵗ˟ⁱᵗⁱᵗ˟ⁱᵗⁱᵗⁱᵗⁱᵗⁱ, ⁱᵗⁱⁱⁱⁱⁱᵗˢᵃⁱᵗⁱ ⁱⁱᵈlⁱⁱᵗⁱ̇

When my grandfather, Abel Frederiksen was alive, he used to tell a story about a hunting trip near Simiutaruaq. He came across three polar bears who had just killed a seal. When they saw my grandfather, they ran away and every so often one of them stood up on his hind legs like a hare to see if they were being pursued. My grandfather said he had never seen anything so magnificent. He brought home the dead seal they had left behind.

I have never been lucky enough to see a polar bear, but once when I was out hunting one on the ice along the Western shore, we came across the tracks of a bear.

16

tássa áma takeîdlôïdlugo simeutarssúp sujetáne upenagssá-
kut átagigaluara Abil Frederiksen avangmut kajartordlu-
ne nanorssuit pingajeiskat takusimavai, ugssuk kenottak
pissarigât takutdlleriartmatik tapikángatermatáme támar-
simavfitik násimariarmássuk pisarssuat tiguinarsima-
vâ, avangmut kimámata takoránermerarsimavai pingajer-
ssuángôt ukatdllitut nikuivdlune assamut narajortulerá-
game piniagagssarssuit pilerinarsimássusê   taimani-
me áma kajainarmik angatdlaterkat Patatdlaramik pisagssa-
kik námagilertaratdliarmatigît.

        uvanga sule nánumik takusiméngîlangatumá-
rarssue takusimavaka avangmut angatártalerrárame
atálákut, lagalugît.

                              Thomas Frederiksen

About thirty years ago, my father bought a motorboat. It was twenty-two feet long and cost only $180. When I first started to fish, we used to go out to the coast near Saattut and fish alongside the fishermen from the Roe Islands. When they fished close to the banks there, they could fill their boats with cod in no time at all.

Those were the times when cod was plentiful. When they finished, their boats were always full. We caught plenty, too, because fishing from a motorboat is a lot easier than from a rowboat.

In the winter, when the fishing season was over, the motorboat gave us a lot more fun, because it was perfect for hunting walruses, seals and white whales. All the time I was a boy, I listened to all the tales about hunting trips and longed for the day when I would be old enough to go along.

1986 me atâtanga pujortulisartârpor 22 fedsimik
1.200 kr. akexarunarpor taimane mêrardlunga ava-
tivtsinut Sûtsumut aulisariartarpungut. ilârxâr-
dlunga Savalingmiormiut kisassimârtut umia-
tsiârtât aulisaxatigisarparut ilâne avunga i-
kardlumut aulisariarâgamik kâjagdlûnardlus-
tik uterarant uligkâvigdlutik.

taimanne sârigdlexaxaox. sôru-
name umiarssuartik uligkâvigdlugo avalâ-
put. ama atâtagkut sârigdligtaxaut. pujor-
tulixaxaledlunime umiatsiânarmik gisaune-
ruvox ama ulkingluit ilualentigusârgut aor-
fit ugssuit xilalugkasdle gisarisarpait ila ti-
kitâgamik oxalugtuât anaimertaxaut uxorna-
kalutigdlo ilâxalimigisax erinimax. kiterpune
urfit xagumasarssimaput tasma-
ne angumeritxarnimanâit. mâna- Thomas Frederiksen
le nânulelavatsle auerpaxsuaxartarpox malerdlugit.

Later on, my father bought another motorboat. It was twenty-two feet long also, but it had a tarpaulin cover over it, which made it better for fishing out in the open sea. The price of boats keeps rising. This new boat cost $1,550.

And it was in this boat that my older brother and I were taught how to sail and fish. Before I started, my brother used to go out and fish with long lines with my father near Saattut. Even in rough weather they would come home with the boat filled to the gunwhales with gutted cod, which they would trade.

åma atåtanga pujottulérartåkigpok avatåsiu-
tåsingnåssumik kinungmat 22 fodsilik kalilikpi-
lingnekarpok ilåne avatåne anorisiutigisarar-
put ajúngenaok orparigkaluarpok 11,000 krume-
karpok agatdllatit akitsoralugtuinaramik.

   Iåssalo perorssåtigisarput imarsiutiku-
minartúngúgame kaleteriatune itorfågdlússa-
kaok, katångutigingrinåvdluta Pitalo angatdla-
ligisarparpuk. sujugdlermik mårågatdlara-
ma angajora atåtangalo nigigtagkerssortarput
avatåne åma såtune pujottulérkåtalo aigpå a-
lotdluarparput taunalo anordleraluartumiturit
såtugdlingmik lisarigkanik siligkårdluge tunini-
åssutigalugo iluarnaok

     Thomas Frederiksen
      Igm.

I was still quite young when I started fishing with long lines in the open sea with my older brother Peter. I remember very vividly the first time we got caught by a southwesterly storm. There were just the two of us and a boy of my age from Attu. At one point, with the wind behind us, we were hit by an enormous wave and nearly capsized. And when we finally managed to get round to the lee side of an island, the boat was half full of water because the tarpaulin cover had been blown off the hatch.

Thomas Frederiksen

inussugtuarángoráma Pítale avatáne nigigtaq
kerssortarpungut, annalo pujortulisarput kaleka-
liúrsoe Avigsersniap avatáne kiángarssuarmut
pukasarditdluta, anorisiorxárnira ilávdluga taimane Aydorninumile inussugtuarxamik ilutiviik
iláissoxarpungut. — sujuydlusmile oxunisigtealuar-
dluta scärdigdluta sangniktätördluta kisaleriter-
dluta (kíngunga japagugdluta) sangniktänaraxta
assummkánxu igerdlavdluta kissukaraxta, oxxu
ijunguit anasakaugut Kästíta matua katauksá-
tigo íoraqsimaxaluta nátagutollo katagardlugit
nikumakaoa atoxxáxdlugo "mássitutdtlo nuine ku xi

7 March 1957

This winter has been unusually mild with good catches of fish. The cold and dark is still noticeable on the return trips home. But with the spring coming, the sun rides high over the western icepack, where many animals are on the move. It is more and more tempting, and as usual, whether it is day or night, we head for there in our beloved motorboat. We are young, eager, always ready to hunt, full of fun and always kidding about.

Our best shot, my 21-year-old brother Peter, steers the boat. I am 17 years old and in charge of the motor. And as a result, I am always dirty. My younger brother Lars, who has just turned 15 and has just started to sail and hunt, is with us as well as another boy almost my age. We have lots of fun, especially the two younger ones. Now and then, they start wrestling. They remind me a little of two big puppies, always testing their strength.

As I write in my journal, it is getting on towards evening. It is twelve hours since we left home, and we are getting near the western icepack.

1957-me ukiok piudluarmartok isse koperdlagdlo kángiúkiat-
tulerssok pissarigssúardluarsimaodluta, avatáne sikotssuit piniagagssarakissut kajugernarsikutórtut, sekinerki-
agtalersimane Mars uletardme únuaru dláta ilerkútitu-
násit pujortulértánguaotinik avangmutárpungut kima-
ta kimakaugut inúsugtuinávugúme piletitotugtorpent akor-
natinilo kuianarlagssar ajornángekaok. — angaj ugdlotsssarput
Pita 21-nik ukiulik autdlánagdlurkigssok (akugtok) nálungari-
gartligo uvangalo akugtúvdlungalo mistaliugama pajakisarpu-
nga 17mik ukiokardlunga nakatalo Lárse 15-ninik ukiulik a-
perssotlimat ilagisulerparput ilausotputdlo Jörgen Rasmusen
ilutiga. ássut sangmisarput tágna Agtormiússok, únag-
ssátniatdlutik ilâne upánagsáput patigtániatdlutik,
ilâme kuianattakat sórdlo nutarkat makeungniúlut.
    lássa uvdlotsiutivne 7 Marts 1957. agdlagsimassok erká-
massata maligdlugo únutersssok sikotssuit kaniqdliter-
dlugit 12 timi igetdlarérdluta.

                        Thomas Frederiksen.
                        Jgn

8 March 1957

Today we shot a fierce walrus and its one year old calf. It is difficult to get near walruses on ice floes with a motorboat, so we always bring a kayak with us. That works well and does not scare the game away. The walrus we shot was almost fully grown and filled the hold of the boat, so we sailed on and reached the open water, about 24 hours from the coast. Our plan is to get to Attu, a small village where we can sell our catch.

9 March 1957

We reached the western icepack. There we sighted white whale and began to hunt it in a rising gale. We caught the whale just before dusk, towed it to the leeside of a small iceberg and hove up there overnight because it was impossible to reach the coast against the north wind.

3 Marts 1937 : igdlâlik puarisartok auveu pisarerput kaunsartararta : luauukigisasârput sikuit akornanêtdut ilâ ne sikut sai mite puilaterpigalugit arnêsarmata kalerêinâ'ngimenugmat. ámu imânarme dengtex pisarerirarligd pisilalabuigut kingmukardlutale sikut akornaxigut igerdlaudlute ãma imartâ timut uvdlormut igerdlasariarox, silesdle siguarmuit puitdlavigisasparut. Agtumutdlo tumiu ãvungut.

9. Mais sikorssait kitdligat tikiparput kilalugarssuan tokulerá'tige anoxdkiteraluartok malerssordlugo pisarerput tairsok kaligdllugo tluliánguip oxuane imuxdvungut aungasigssuak timukatpliingimat.

10 March 1957

When the terrifying stormy night was over and dawn came, we saw that huge ice floes had been broken into small pieces. We did find an ice floe large enough to haul the white whale on to and flenshed its hide off. We left the meat behind it had gone bad from being in the water too long. My older brother knew the way to our destination very well, so we had already begun to estimate what time we would arrive as we stood on the ice cutting the blubber from the whale's hide.

As we sailed on between the ice flows we caught two more walruses, and now the motorboat was full to overflowing. But we were now getting closer to the coast. The weather started to change, however, with a cold air from the north replacing the calm.

ínuak amilánnartok kåg:upoksunaussa tugdligssa ajorner uv-
dlángorpok atorsarordlunilo kisiangne sikut serumissimakaut
puloleltordluta putak amasiofisinaussok tiki kavtigo pilag-
tigárput pujortulárkavtínipok erne, J. Rasmusen, uvanga. Pitáru.
kartaralo putamipungut. matå orssúalonerálo uligkárutigárut
áma neka utornasimanermik kajortisimagame lamå tigú-
ngilarput ámame serusumik kaligkáttye putdlagtisimagame.
        uligkáravla kivigajayodluta límakerpugut 10 Mars
áma siko sinerdlugo aortit mardluk pisarigátigit nuá-
nerawr kåtsuganerssuak imisáraluardlune nunaka-
nigdligipuldlo tåtsivdlune avángasigásit suersiartotpok
orkartugságavlale ajungilak angajugdlersátalo arku-
lå nalúngeringmago matål orssúialerpagut tikiotissar-
put erkorrarérdlugo.

Thomas Frederiksen
Iginiarfik.

11 March 1957

It is before daybreak on the morning of King Frederik IX's birthday. While my older brother was steering the boat, all of a sudden there was a crash. We had hit a reef. The boat started to keel steeply over, and we were all thrown to one side. Right away, we started to throw our load overboard. But the skin of the walrus on top got caught, jamming the opening of the hold and could not be moved. We were in shallow water and even with the motor going we could not get refloated. There would be a long wait for the tide. We took turns in standing watch. All of a sudden I noticed that water was getting in at the stern of the boat, and the pieces of whale blubber on the deck were being washed away. Since everything looked so hopeless, I suggested to my older brother that he should ferry us one at a time to the nearest island on the kayak. And if we could not balance on the deck of the kayak, he should tow us in the water. We knew we were now in real trouble and were very nervous. Nobody wanted to be first, so I volunteered. When we reached land, I was freezing cold from the icy water. And as I stood there on the little island and waited for the others, all of a sudden I felt terribly lonely.

11 Marts 1957

11 Marts kúnge Frederik IX imúvigsrottok uvdlágssakut 1957
pingasúvdlutá otsuiávunqut angajugdleissarput akugtok tārsi-
simaleretssok nunat akormanut pulámākavto igerdlaniardlu-
ta lássóngainarssuak kángottordlo pisotpalugssack kisimiuvox
misigilétpunqut igdluinánut piotardlutá ikardlípungut uve-
rajugssuardluta, - etkániataluarpungut aotfitdle amerssue kag-
dliugamik uvertugutdlo tátokiússimagamik ajornakaut. nal.20
kardlípungut linimörpok liníngakaotdle maskinamik kángatniatalu-
arétavta unitinarparpul initáne isersimárpungut akaantlo sisuertor-
dluta kagdlutíngisámat kujanakaotdle anore inotiatkotmal. nal.20
ulimúlerpok anorsatigsiartorkilerpok akua alagkatatdletiga os-
ssut sávigalersimasut akua agpardlune kagdlúsimavox kiviar-
tulerdlutalo nal.24. ilagka okatfigáka okua imarssuarmik uligkár-
dimavox. Pilap akivánga "kalokiuk" akivara, kiviartulerpungut kagdlúsi-
magátla" nagdlartitinartox okatfigára "ikunga kekertárkemúltkásotniar-
liqut kairamik usiarsinángikútigut kaligtéssuátigut" káu rap kilerutépe-
tiarpra kangale pétérpai agdlamut sápunga kisatdlungalo ilagka sker-
lugsátúsimasut uvanga ikinakága kagalenigdláydlak unorkigsárdlug-
kettátánguamat iketevérdlugalo aitsat kiserdliiumeralua spunge manuss

12 March 1957

Alone on that little island, I felt completely helpless. My legs felt heavy, and my clothes started to freeze. Thinking that maybe I would be the only one to be saved, I went on my knees and raised my clasped hands towards heaven in anxiety. When the others finally did reach the island, I was not only relieved but felt stronger. We were young and strong, and it was our duty to look after our parents and serve our country well.

My older brother gave us a pair of oars and some of the blubber to eat, and then set off towards Attu, without his parka because it had been lost in the sea. We remained on the island, wet, thirsty and sleepless. We started to run to keep warm. I could feel that the wind was rising. The others were getting nervous, and were beginning to feel drowsy. I knew it would be fatal to sleep in such cold, and so I did my utmost to keep them awake. My younger brother, the other boy and myself started to run and wrestle again to keep warm.

When the two boys seemed happier, I walked away from them and prayed to God that he would protect my brother who was trying to get help in the kayak. After that, I felt my strength come back. Soon it was possible to make out the half-sunken motorboat. And at daybreak we heard engine noise, which then faded away. A little later we saw a motorboat on the way from Aqisserniaq. It was "Margrethe" with the priest who was on service calls. A little later, it returned with another boat, "Karlsen." Our motorboat was raised and tied between the two larger boats. Before long, we were safe in Attu.

32

17/3 Sivieeertáránguamut pingama angnikildlúmeraga niuheleve
nákaul masakigama atisákalo kerrutilerdlutik, ilánguagka a-
junássagaluatpata etkánek sapetavko kisima ánagtúnigssata sérku-
ngmetpuga "únerssuivdlugalo,, ilalo erkigsiatdlakauga ilánguag-
kalamatmik ikármata inúsagtúvugúme angajotkágut nunar-
putdlo suligesuniagagssaralugit "ánersákuldlo nunappissáneta-
la kánipungut Gulivdle áissaisa pissaissuit atánigdluta...!

Pilap maglangmik takugsserdluta nanertuarfétardlo ipu-
liedlo mardluk niórtiardlugit Agluliardlune káinamik autdlatpox a-
norssarigsisotssávox arkutigssálo sarfakalune akuilesakángi-
lax nákasunut ilávdlune sáuigsimangmat, uvagutdlo masakaluta
siningitórtarsimavdluta imetusokalutali kerkertáránguar kávig-
dlugo únagsárpagut suersigalugtuinarmat ilánguagka etnumaler-
gut malugaka ináratusogtutdlo ekersatdlugit issekingmat ilingitá-
kinangmata okalúgpavka ilauserrputdlo nikatdliorkajánetsávox a-
ngajúgdletsáta kajánigsánik okalugdlune iniliormiattuinar nu-
kartátalo arpaliugtialetátine únalerdlune okarpox "nukarigssáinássit,,
okatsrigáka "áitsál patigtáusisángotpox patigtániatilik,, patitátukesingeti-
atamik kisa igdlattalerput "ajungakáng itsamut sernigerkuara ilánguagkalo tikikikáikit nuáná-
kauga sórdlume akuerinerkartunge. avatiotine pujottulérak kives
kasox etsilárdlunilúna nukattátalo tátseokarpox "sórdlo sing nagtuku-
tórssuax. kisa káumarsimalersox lukutótpalugsiulerpungut taimagálo
nipáruvdlane kijorna Akigserniáptungánik etserpox sunáuvá kargaethe,
Palase agatdlagdlugo Agtumitek námagtórsimagá Akigserniamutdle ikikitligsáso-
simasut Karlsenip Margrithiodle akornáne pujottulérae simárparput. Agtumut ilúmik p-
nekagátpungei

April 1957

Since our accident in March, we continued our hunting expeditions with great success. On April 10th, after we had been to the Bay of Disko, we sailed out from the coast out towards the western icepack. But when the northern wind got stronger, we turned around and made harbour in Attu. We knew that several boats were still out: "Margarethe," "Karlsen," "Ujarlilooq" ("Forever Searching") and "Angerlartorsuaq" ("the one named after a deceased"). On April 11th the north wind was still rising, approaching hurricane force. On April 13th we heard the crew of the "Karlsen" on the radio, reporting they had reached Itilleq, south of Holsteinborg. We immediately asked if the other boats from Aqisserniaq had reached port, but were told there was still no sign of them. By April 14th, "Margarethe" had still not arrived home at Iginniarfik (the bird hunting area). But shortly afterwards, we heard that "Margarethe" and "Ujarlilooq" had reached Itilleq. "Angerlartorsuaq" had sunk, but the crew had been saved by the "Margarethe." Another boat, the "Elsinore" had been forced aground on Sukkertoppen (The Sugar Top) and two other boats from Itilleq and Sarfannguaq had disappeared with their crews.

This drawing shows "Margarethe," with "Ujarlilooq" nearby, picking up the crew from "Angerlartorsuaq" which is only a 20 foot boat and very old. The rescue took place shortly before the hurricane arrived.

34

1957 upernagssagkut umiagajangnita kigatna pisaramevdluarpavngut angalattuardlutalo Diskobugtimutagdlat angalarerdluta 10 Abril avangmukatalu atdlule avangnarkanangnersuerssatuinarmat Agtumut pinaravta numarkatigut Margrithe,, kut Jkrgsermermiutdlo "Karlsen,, "Ujardlilör,, "Angerdlartorssuardlo,, Avangmukarsimaput Agtumitangut 11 Abril avangner suerpok ama akagukut anoerssuartlotssuvek 13–u "Karlsen,, Jkidlimut nunisimavdlane numarkatilik tikisimanasualugit radidkut tusarmarpai Jkrgsermermat tusarniavungut tikisimangitdlatdle ama 14 Abril Jgimiarfingmut ama "Margrithe,, pitarutingitsersgimavek tauvale radiskut tusaterpangut Jkidlimut nunisimassut "Margrithe,, "Ujardlilör,, dle Angerdlartorssuak, kivisimavek inuile Margrithemut tkisimeput tamarmig dle ajsatik "Elsenörte, Janitsumut nunisimavek ravunga Jkidlimiutdle sartanguarmiutdlo ajunarsimaput pajertuterkat mardia

       kulene Pitertqungara tassa "Margrithi,,p Angerdlartorssuak, pilugsimavdlugo tsukartarnersingmat sajuutapiluvto nusugdlugo kivisiartutermat rave ikrinalerat, imakame riugatinarpat angaldlatinguek pisavak 20 Pedsilik timakarnermene atanaviangitaluarmat anoerssuarme 12 nik nakugssasilingme ánausinternek ama riugerssunássakringame inaisaanaunigsaut pingarnetungame kujanavak nalivtine ajunartekangitkatdlatame, tautkule anoetessuatmile ajugavtiyinekatkut netsernakissut kingulingue misingengnekatiginekut tássaupume uvavtitkut pitersagagdlit sujunigsamile nerriutekertut ajernakaerdle angaldlat angisetssugaluartek imarssup atkungita sulile pissaunekarpek,, tamakume atortitajut pivdluarnermut avkutigssatut ka, Thomas Frederiksen

Lätdlit ama navianartortutuwite isugumasgngitdlat skutkumatumat imumertik sujulivtutut sloatinsarkgo

4 May 1957

We enjoyed wonderful weather in Diskobugten, the Bay of Disko, while we were hunting a shoal of white whales. The government health department boat "Bjarnov" and another boat from Nivaaq came along for company. Doctor Olsen was on his way to Angissat to treat a patient on the summer hunting ground, and took part in the whale hunt. But his shots were far too low to hit the whales.

We shot two when the whales came up right in front of our boat. After harpooning, we killed the largest of the two. Olerujuk (Big Ole) from Nivaaq in the third boat killed the other one we had shot. With the help from one of the sailors from the health department boat, we flayed our catch on an ice floe. After that we shared the meat of the two whales between the three boats.

The summer in Diskobugten can be beautiful, but now and then there will be some fierce storms in the fall, when there is a risk of being iced over. Great care is necessary, and it is important to know all the emergency harbours.

4 Maj 1957. Diskobugtime alianaik kilalungarpovssuit nāmē-
tēravligit materssulerssungut "Bjarnow", Nivârmiut ardlata-
tugit tikiúput sunâvfa Agissanitsut nápatsimasotlakar-
mata nakotseg Olsen-ip takusarsimagai tássamiássit ā-
ma serkotatausatpok inersaruinarame.

larma ne sujuninguatotátigut mardluk aut-
dlágavl.igit pisaŕávut angrssok kalusiugtátigo nāle-
rétdlugo Olsenujugkut Ni-Niâtmiut isottak attutersi-
tatput namavdlugó nagíkaut pilagpungut "Bjarnow,
p kivfāsa ilât rkiotsiuvdlugo ilagut tikiungmata avgu-
atpagut kilalugkat mardluk angatdlat.it pungasivdlu-
ko nuánekaok mánato sila alianaik. aussame āma
alianágtaxaok. autisagaxaxalumilo. Diskobugt ilámile t-
mánānginvigtsumik anot. Thomas-Fredirksen
dlurtarpok sualungmilo u-
kiáleut. sianisáxnastaxaok   Ign.
unniatsialinitdlle nalunagit kimâriarfigalugit
agungiverusaraluarput. nalundrdlumik korsoka
jârnartarpok sualungmik nunat agssuane
silkut exciteritset oxungleuninastānginkalinka-
kait. sexatordlutik iqusorsixaxamik

The winter of 1958 was very good for the seal hunt. At times we would have up to 18 seals in our house. We three brothers caught seals in Alanngorsuak, a fjord that never froze because of a strong current. Every day we drove 5 miles in a dogsleigh to get there. My father, Jorgen Frederiksen, caught a lot of seals by net; in three months we caught about 200. My mother Regina, who was the district midwife, was untiring in looking after our catch. Only our sister was too young to help. Our young brother and three of his friends helped, and also went out hunting when they had a day off from school. Everybody in the district caught plenty of seals.

As long as the ice pack is close to Attu and Kangaatsiaq there is always good hunting in the district.

Thomas F.

1958 ukiorʌ pitsak sikorʌnaorʌ puisʌsʌavalunilʌ uvdluk
ilånʌ puisʌt 18 igdluʌtʌmut kiteʌitarpavut uvangut ka-
tångutigik puingasuʌvdluta Alångorʌsuarʌmut anguni-
artarpungut kilʌrdlitit umiatsialʌsimasarpungut I-
giniʌarfingʌmut km 8 simugʌserʌtarpungut nuimʌr-
tarʌaorʌ aunʌ atåtanga Jörgen Frederiksʌn napituʌarʌaorʌ
uvdlormut ilånʌ 8 kiteʌitarpäi ʌaumatinʌ puingasu-
nʌ 200 erʌänʌ puisʌsitaʌävut anänarput nʌrsʌmaʌaorʌ
Jumʌujusorʌ Igiʌniʌarfingʌmʌ Rʌgʌnʌ Frederiksʌn anguta-
narssʌssʌgut ikʌiorʌʌnarpätigut arʌmartaduasput
mirʌägamʌ nukagpiarʌkatʌllʌ puingasʌut ilʌnʌʌutärʌi-
sʌartarput ilånʌsʌugtaʌvalukʌigʌllʌ atʌmångiʌarfingʌmʌ-
rʌʌ nunaʌʌʌatigut ämʌ pisʌaʌʌardluʌartarput erʌʌä-
minguʌtʌllʌ. Agʌto. Kangåtsiʌardlʌ puʌartaʌʌaut sʌʌa-
lunʌmilʌ avʌatäi sikorʌtulʌåʌinʌastaʌʌmik

October 1958

We sometimes go into Nassuttooq, the north part of Stromfjord, to trap fox. On October 30th I trapped a white fox and a blue fox. It is always great to hunt. In November, when we arrived home from the hunt we had caught 1 seal, 13 foxes, 2 hares, 1 skaru, 63 eiderbirds, and 7 puffins. On most hunting trips there are usually some hardships, but we tend to recall the good times the most. In the spring, as long as the ice is safe, we can use the dogsleigh to check our fox traps. During a summer with little bad weather, you always catch many more foxes. Fox hunting is always exciting, but can also be exhausting, especially if there is a lot of snow.

OKTOBER 1958 Nagsugtúmut teriangniarniaravta puldlaser-
soriartordluta tássane kakortak kernerdlo pisaráka 30
OKT. nuánekaok angalárdlune Novemberimilo titkipungut
pisarisimavdlugil natsigdlat 1 teriangnigssat 13 ukatdlit2
okaitsok 1 merkit 63 agpat 7, áma pissanganartokartat-
pok angalanerup nagsatarisertagánik nuánekutásunig-
dlo erdlakilártardlunime nuánetssok kaningnerusarpok
upernagssakut kaimugsimik puldlaciartarput siko aug-
dlune atugagssajúnártínago au. Thomas Frederiksen
esákut silardlúlkajugpatdlángskangat
teriangmaukenerusarpok. nuánekawaok iláme agutekarpat
dláságame scasínahajórtaralunpu.

17 February 1959

The Strait of Alanngorsuaq is slow to freeze over because of a strong current. At last, it has frozen. Every winter we ferry travellers by sleigh to Niaqornaarsuk a village on the other side. This year we took two policemen, an Eskimo and a Dane, over the frozen strait without a boat. Because it was very cold, they did not have their uniforms on.

To freight people, dogs and equipment by boat in extreme cold can be very dangerous, and calls for great skill and care. It can be extremely hazardous when boats ice over, especially at night. Think that in the old days hide-covered women's boats were used for freighting. Sometimes we sailed in freezing fog and could not see a thing, and the only way to navigate was to sail by the direction of the wind.

In large open areas in the ice large flocks of seabirds congregate. All the birds we used to catch there were a good supplement to our winter food stocks. When I see those seabirds in these openings in the ice, I always think of a legend about the great hunter Qattaaq, who went out to catch eiderbirds far from the coast.

Thomas Fr.

17 Februar, 1939. Aláñgôtssuan utkiut 35 sikasimanane si-
kuldlarmat. atortdíngnik ángaláttunik ikássuilôrtardluta kisame Niaket nárssangmik kimugseit nangminek ikárput tássa Politit kalálen naydlunárdlo Ukal,iik aláñgorkuvdluga Tasi-
ussárssúp Pungánut ingerdlártut. Politítut Undiformenkaralik issingmat
       baimátuánar tássegaluaramik ikássuinek imartúngska-
luarlox iláne sianisárnartakigame pujoragssuak iláne ser-
mernartakigame sikualuntále anerdlersume tánsitivdluge
apernajánartakigamik sikunialitdlarmat sule ikássuinek at-
Zórnar netuterame iláme sermernek isse ajutôraluat útale
uvangut akisugsártígaluget ikátagul ále sujugdlermik umiamik
ikássuisarsimasut. likardluqule ajúngilax pujoragenuarme ava-
lagkágauta okunigdluta apútilíssanguit ássordlutasonnap tugánik
anorisártuartarame uvilenitorágat nunanile ersitsonáreyi-
kaluartox nalunarnek Thomas Frederiksen
ajorpox sumulvagssavdlume.
              Ign.
    sikokingmat merkitangmalagtisut pisárutígávut imar-
nersatuánguit tingmiarugssat imarmiut najorniartaking-
matigil erkárkajánerpok "Kátákut mitermiarnerat.

It is said that Qattaaq always was an eager hunter, even when he was old. Once when the sea was frozen over, he climbed to the top of a nearby hill to look out for the possibility of a catch. Far out on the ice he noticed frost fog rising from a couple of places.

Early the next morning he took off with his two sons and a stepson. Far out from the shore they discovered a hole in the ice where there were plenty of eiderbirds. After a while they realized that they had caught so many that they would have to stop. But on the way back to the coast they noticed that the ice floes they were crossing had started to drift out. Obviously a storm was brewing.

Kûlârik utorkakasi uvdlune pilerîtoraok ilânigôk sikutdlat-
mat karkat portunersiviardlugit nasigkame tasamaner-
ssuar pajotatat ûgaletisugartutlakuai.

'ŝletame avangmel eragukul ernine mardlut einersienilerin
galugit sagdlerânguit kapísimalerdlugit imarnereaktikepâl
miterpessuit nuanersiseritotât utorkartât pikerpok "naysalegssuse kivi-
arsigit,, tauvamuko nangmâssutik sivnitivdlardlugit. lunungmukar-
niardlutik nunasarnetssuarmik sívitâpat.

They were driven out to sea and eventually landed at Akilineq on the coast of Canada. There the stepson was killed by a stranger during an armwrestling contest. Qattaaq challenged the murderer, defeated him, and then killed him. Later they found out that the stranger always killed his guests.

Qattaaq always wore a lemming as an amulet. The lemming saved their lives and even brought the stepson back to life. After that, they met a witch, who tried to bewitch them so they would die. But when Qattaaq and his sons also wore pieces of bearskin as amulets, these enabled them to jump into the sea and take on the form of three polarbears.

When the stepson, who wore a snowsparrow as an amulet, was afraid of being left behind, the bears shouted "Why don't you use your small wings or else the witch Apiakasik will take you." And all of a sudden he was transformed into a snowsparrow. So they were all able to get back over the sea and reached home safely.

ui̇sȧgamik savilȧput akiliṅermutdlopiṅgamik er-
nersiaᵵa Akiliṅermiorssuak pakȧsuṅgmika ig̊suersipor-
dle aṅguᵵisialo sagsarame ᵵanarssuakasik ᵵorȧupȧ. sunauᴵ-
ᵵa ᵵekuȧrᵵiminik ûmaᵵiᵵasarsimȧngiᵵsoe ᵗunangmisarᵵorssuak.

ernetsiane ûmaᵵeserȧmiuk aviṅgȧᵵime anȧmaᵵik kima-
put Apiakasik puᵵusukasiṅgormaᵵ nanoraminȧᵵsianig̊dloȧᵵnu-
akaᵵamik nanûṅgordluᵵik imȧnuᵵ ᵵerkȧpuᵵ ernersiȧlekū-
paloᵵaᵵsûṅguamik ȧrnualik nagalermaᵵ avaᵵȧne nanorssu-
ᵵ ᵵordluᵵȧkauᵵ. Apiakasip neᵵinȧssakauᵵiᵵ sisoriaᵵdluᵵiᵵ isaᵵ-
kilagaluaᵵiᵵ, kupaᵵoᵵaᵵosûṅgormaᵵ ikȧrput.

9 March 1959

Outside our hamlet, where I go ice fishing, I caught 23 flounders, 2 isinger, 1 crab and 1 skolast. Small flounders are useful for feeding the dogs. But since they are very tasty, we often eat them as a change from our daily diet of seal meat. Travellers passing through our hamlet also buy food for their dogs. For a short while the Royal Greenland Trading Company tried trading flounders but they soon gave that up when they realized that trading in seal meat paid a lot better for the hunters. Methods of hunting and fishing are always being changed and improved to suit local conditions. At our hamlet we have been using "gliders" to lay down our long fishing lines under the ice. A hole is made in the ice, and a square metal plate with extra weights on it is dropped into the water. The "glider" drifts through the water and reaches the bottom far away from the hole, so the rest of the fishing line with the hooks on it is drawn gradually after it and in that way is stretched out over the floor of the sea without being tangled.

Thomas Fr.

9 Marts 1959 ikivtine kaleralingniartunga taimane
23 årpunga anûtat2 sãtuak 'saviuvdlopûa, pisatôke.
kaleralerkat kingminul nerisaiitivdlugit iluakaut
ãmame mamakigamik nekinut avdlanissutausaramik
angalasutdlume piumawaut kingminut netukautigisa-
ramigkik. ilãme ãkajâkasiussarput tunisãtsiaraluer-
put akikitsûvdlutigdle, Handelimik misilingnewata-
luatame tg angumiatkunekartut angúngitsôrpait
iluamit sangminekánginamik puisingniartner sang
minekarnetugame pingârtumik kagsuserssotnek
akigssatsinarnetungmat.

Thomas Frederiksen

Igr.

sutdlûnit piniarnume anlisarnermile nagssajus-
ssut aikusartume, sikeumu ajortumile iluacutãsa-
kait nalenutlungerssagâgamik atornewalernermini-
lo iluarsiartortardlutit. uvant sãrdlisãtok ator-
newarpoк ᵃ sike puteriardluge kigdlertoramunu o-
rimalutilatererluge migrimuartarput ᵃ sãrdlisãtok
tiggpat uminyatilanardluge, kisitã dutit artumidluge.

1 May 1959

Here we are seen hunting white whales in the Bay of Disko
north of Ikamiut beyond Upernavik. While we were on shore
on lookout, a hunter by the name of Johan from Ikamiut
came by on his dogsleigh. It was a beautiful day with a warm
spring sun. We sat down and cooked seal meat over a fire
while he entertained us with exciting tales. However, since we
were in an area where there always were lots of white whales,
we continued to keep watch over the sea. By May 3rd we
were able to take home to Iginniarfik the remains of 22
white whales. We had an abundance of wonderful tasty
blubber.

Towards the east the Tussaaq Island is visible. Over to the
left behind the icebergs is Qasigiannguit (Christianhaab),
where there are several shrimp beds, and also plenty of big
tasty sea cats. Lots of cod can be caught near the icebergs.
But you have to fish with great caution near the icebergs,
because they are inclined to keel over very suddenly.

50

1 Maj 1955 Diskobugdeme kilalungarmerdluta Ikamiut a-
vangnâne Upernavingme alianaekisox nasigdlute Ikami-
ormiox suât tikiungmat kimugsimik oxaluasâtlox lusar-
nâsutigalugo nekitûpungut igavdluta kiniutigalugo kila-
lugaxalexinangmat ila alianaxk sexinex kialâtssuax ma-
nalo issikivigik nuân. —

    3 Maj Iginiarfingmut angerdlarpungut kilalug-
xat alautixôxtat 22 pisaxaxalâxfigalugit mâtangungnânge-
xaox.

                Thomas Frederiksen Iginiarfik.

kagivtine xaxigiâxgut nunâ ilulias-   Dr Egm.
ssuit nalâne assilissup talexpialugâne xexertax
Tugssax ersipox. tamâna xagia xâjaxaxfuxaxpox
Upernivinp xalôxfia anerdlaxissunik, âma xexa-
xarfigpaxssuaxaxtox inmixa nalinguxait mâ-
leulo nexpigik. ilulixarssuitollo xxxait xâxug-
dlit nuânarinaxait uloxianalâxinxxtaxannik au-
lisarfigalugit axxoxiatâxsinâxaxanik.

7 May 1959

A long way from the shore, we came upon a herd of walruses.
After killing six, we had no more room in the boat, so we
sailed home. And on the way back we passed a big shoal
of white whales. With a motorboat as small as ours, we can
only do so much hunting.

As we neared the coast we were surprised by a northern storm.
But we reached Attu safely. Sailing through a storm, every-
one has certain duties that have to be performed, no matter
how tired one is. Sailing past icebergs demands special care.
If they are aground, or if they are beginning to break up,
one should always sail by on the leeward side, since the water
on the windward side is usually rough and can be full of
small icebergs that are very dangerous for a boat.

7 Maj 1959. avatäne auverpavssuit tikipangut arfinierär-
pungut uligkäriarférurdluta ímerarta tímakänakaugut
äma wilatangatparvssuit nämätoraluarpavut ímatku-
kinipalakasik-ä·,, igitakängitaguidle.

nunakanigdligipaidle äma avängasiup errorlormiat-
satilerpätigut ímerartinaraox sarfak majorásaglor-
ssügame apäidluätpunguidle Rytumat. anorisiulerww-
dlune imigissare suliar-   Thoma Frederiksen
dle wimangnaoisrärtari.
acarput! wasngaluaränilümit, imarisasügäine kiä-   Igu.
nik ipiydlugo! wärtigdlumilo nigdlägdllagkägäme
kanga ilosfägdl! - äma awngdlune maliarasuit
wärmeriwortumerit agssorwungniartariauartarput!
sikutdle alcorrämgdlune ilulissat ikerdllrimarut
agssorwungniartariakängitdllat! sarfarvingdlümit. ₒ

29 May 1959

Once while I was in the Amerloq area south of Sisimuit, along with my younger brother Lars, we rescued a Dane. His motorboat had been grounded because of engine trouble and now was being driven towards the coast by a very strong wind. We towed him home to the hamlet Sarfannguaq, where he lived.

At that time the cod industry was declining. Only in very deep waters were cod still plentiful, and these we caught with long lines.

1 June 1959

At 9:30 p.m. on a beautiful evening we set out from Sisimiut along with Jens Geisler and his boat Aaveq (The Walrus). The next day at 3:00 p.m. we reached Iginniarfik to attend the confirmation of our only sister, Magdaline Frederiksen.

Aaveq was the first large fishing cutter with a harpoon canon for hunting whales. Jen and his brothers are pioneers in hunting from larger boats, and have inspired many other northern Eskimos to follow suit.

29 Maj 1959 navane Amerdlumigdluta larsilo navdlunåe pu-
joptuléråtnamik uniglorsimavdlune tiputåletssok Sartångu-
aliåpatpule sunaufa Sisimiormio navdlunåe nunasini-
tox. tarmane sujornatigornik sarugdlenardluangineru-
vox ajunångilangutdle nigigtagnerssortlarpungut.

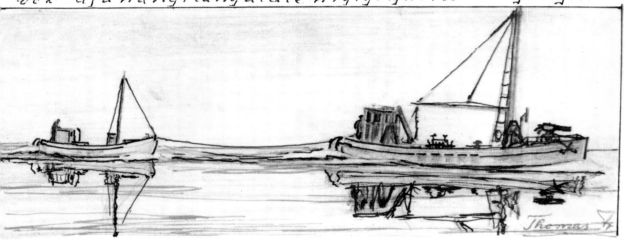

1 June 1959 imugnut nal.9½ Sisimiunik autdlarpungut Jens
Giesler-ip angatdlatå "Awex, igranatigaluga alianaik anvangu-
nut nal.15: Iginartingmut tikipungut arnantetuarputaper-
ssertitox. Magdalene Frederiksen. Awex. pujortulimat namu-
tiligdlit sujagdleresaråt, numaotine pimarnurnvdle
tuvätigut takutitsisuvdluartuvox! Jens natamqutal-
entitå aulavintsut sulvarnurtdlo timivionarnurli-

1959

In the months of July and August there is still plenty of cod on the fishing banks, where we used to fish. A fully-loaded boat holds about 4,000 pounds of cod, which can be sold. Here we are shown at the "bank" fishing along-side "Jenskarl," "Skoburn," "Franz," "200" and "Margrethe."

Sometimes the sea can be completely calm like this. But cod are most plentiful when the current is the strongest and the sea is rough. Storskraapen, the seagulls, always appear where the shoals of cod are. It takes three hours to get out to the fishing banks, they are six miles from our hamlet.

When the cod season is over, we fish for seacats with long lines at Saattut until October. And a long way offshore are the flounder banks where there is always an abundance of fish. Towards the end of autumn when we start hunting seabirds around the fishing banks, we sometimes sail through large shoals of cod close to the surface, and some-times large shoals of salmon.

1959. Juli Augustsk avatitsline skaner ekardierdlo
sårugdlerastararok. aulitsåtarpangut uvangut 2 Tons
erisåne kitusisarpungut.

    uvangut "Jens Karl, "Skodien, "Franz, "Nrza, Margnthe. lo
skamer mitangut. avatä islåne taimäitaråluarpeit mag-
dierdlumile sarfångdiumilo sårugdlenarnerusarpeit pinjar-
tumik katsijusarat tivdiane

                Thomas Frederiksen
                    Jgn.

sårugdlit akuldlaråingato Såtune ararmastarpangut
Otioberemut niggstagarssortarpungut tamarmik J-
kardlerdlo 6 milit migssänigput 3 iune uvangut ornigtarpa-
vut nunavtinik. taijäna Store Hellefiske Banka avaterput, au-
lisagararfigssiuvar sangale, islåne agpangniardlu-
ta ukiålsut ik.åmerssissorimiardlugit agpaluiåstiv-
nerit sumårfalsulca sårugdlit. igerdlartut, å-
ma taimangnagajala kapisigdlit igerdläit to-
kunerartarsimagput Karsjerdlugssup Arfersiorfiup
påtunåne pigssigartorartarsimässdle ukiålsut.

12 December 1959

In the late fall, some blackside seals come into Alanngorsuaq Fjord. From November until February the seal hunt is always good, both from land and from motorboat. Here, I just have shot a formidable seal cow from land. On the other side of the hill my father is in hiding and has also shot one. The same day, my brothers shot several from the motorboat. Large herds of seal can often be seen in the Fjords. In the old days, we used to hunt from kayaks. Kayaks are still used, but mostly by the hunters from Niaqornaarsuk. We get a good price for the blubber and the pelts of the seals we catch. But nobody buys the meat, so it is shared amongst everybody at the hamlet.

12 December 1959, utiagkut atârssuit Alángotssuak pula-
sarpaut. Novembertimik ilâne Februarimut, pujortulêrka-
mik nunamigdlopiniarnekartarput. — tássa Nûgssuarme
Tasiusârssup avangnâlungane, namavdlunga atâk igdlâ-
zik pisarigínga, táimane áma atâtanga kujatâlungí-
ne anguver, igdlâlingmik áma nagka pujortulêrka-
mik angusimapul, imak ikera amisokartaraoi-
sujugdlermik káunamik piniarnekartarput. sulime káunat atornenaraut pingârtumik Niakotnârssungmiu-
nik. Alányorassuarme kapuinariajungnârsaluartut pu-
magagssat sule! Thomas Frederiksen
natssucastanaoir.
nunat nûgajugtat kangmavigssarjuavsuanar-
put, agisumik agatslangmik inigsititeralumilo.
pulagtarfiútigisumik pucartúpat. sikorssuarne-
lúmit ilunanulârnoianoic avatáme

29 December 1959

At the Bay of Nuussuaq, during a grouse shoot, I shot 19 birds and ran out of bullets. There were many more grouse, but it was difficult to get near them because of the deep and soft snow.

When the weather is good, it is a joy to go grouse shooting. In the fall or the spring there are usually many grouse near the Fjord. Some people go grouse shooting with their dogsleighs and shoot a lot of game. But usually it is only the boys that shoot. But teachers and other employed people go grouse shooting, too, in their spare time.

Thomas Fr.

29 Dec. 1958.

uvdlume Nûgssup kangerdlumarnane aeig-
serniarama 19.-ârdlungala nungútigama aeig-
sivararor aputdlo mâsararnarkalune.

Thomas Frederiksen
Igimiarfik

aeigsserpavovsuit ukialeut upernagssâleutdllo ka-
ngerdlungne igerdlâstarput. kimagaimigdlo piniar-
niaráne nâlârdlugit pisavarnartarsimavaror, aut-
dlainiardlumile avângusivârsfinssângevaror sila-
yigtivedlugo kiaisa piniartarniaráne agdlatütdle ä-
ma lunisâvdluarvuvlersimáváput, aulaqparvat a-
eigsserniarajugneruvsaramik. ayovtotle atoroqdlglijtdllo si-
ngiõfinginine piniardlugit viánarisavavt.

February 1960

In Oqaatsut we catch seals with nets under the ice. Here I have just pulled up my catch through the ice. When the net is straightened out, it will be let go down under the ice again. In north Greenland that is the method they use. But out on the open waters in the Fjord we catch from the motorboat, using heavier sea nets with good results.

Oqaatsut Island lies on the other side of Tasiusarsuaq, the great inland lake. In the winter, when the Fjord freezes, we usually move our motorboat to Qiterleq, in the middle, which never freezes because of the strong current.

Thomas Fr.

1960 Februar.

Oxaitsune napitortarpungut imamile pu-
portuliskamik angusardluta tássa napitortara ig-
dlusürdlungit kagssutit ámutigkut amuänardlu-
git siástarput igarai suydlusürdlungit näkäriänä-
ngortisimärdlugit oxaitsut Tasiussärssüp akiáni-
put ukiukut umiatsialisimasarfiata sikugärngat kóter-
dlermut nularpungut.   Thomas Frederiksen

     Avangnäne sikukut kagssuserisomik atorne-
kartaraox. Sikunerdle ajortune imarsiutit, ä-
ma pisavarmastarsimaxait kagssuserfinüdlis-
artune.   puisit igerdläsfiäne ikinäärka-nünüt
kapisiligtät äma puisit talusarfinartarput

2 May 1960

Yesterday we started out from Attu. Along the ice pack west of the Uummannaq Island we caught 2 walruses, 2 ring seals, a newborn ring seal and several puffins.

At this time of the year the catch is abundant in our area. In spite of that, we are sailing south to catch cod. It was foggy when I went to bed. My brother Peter and our passenger, who was also the pilot, sailed the boat. When they later woke me to relieve them they were satisfied that we had made good progress. And when the fog disappeared, I recognized the coast. Palasip-qaqqaa (The Priest Mountain) and Nasaasaaq (The Bitch's hat). They were unmistakable. The wind was strong and our fuel reserves were running low, so I suggested we go into Sisimiut. The other two said together, "But we passed Sisimiut a long time ago." "Look here," I started to explain: "in there I can see Palasipqaqqaa, and back there you can see Nasaasaaq, and now we are passing Qassit Island, which is mentioned in the saga as the island where the great killer Qaassuk lived." Our pilot looked confused. Peter just said, "Why don't you go closer to the coast?" But because of the strong side wind the boat was now rocking heavily. Our dory was on top of the deck, and survived only because it was well tied down.

I can't stop thinking of sagas about the kayaks from Amerloq. In a bad storm, the hunters were forced to land on the island of Qassit, exactly where their great and most feared enemy Qaassuk lived.

igpagssar Agtumik auldlarpungut. Umanap sisiúne sikorssuarne aotfii mardluk pisarigaotigit natsitdlo 2 natsiakasigdlo 1 agparpaluitdlo.

piniagagsálear natúnátugdet Totásit avatorput kujatánat aulisarsínakaugut sárugdlit erkámelerdlugit uvnuat putsilerser ínatama Péta ilausorpatdlo ilisimasortarisarput ilulige arugdlat pârdlarkariarmata arautorpunga pilertornertlut etsilersimangmat nuna ilisarnágdlat "palasip karkâ" Nasaussárdlo sördle kisimik lakotkusul ingerdlaviat kujangmut torkarsimátaluardlugulo sulârput mitdlingmat áma anorsarekingmat apetáka sisimiunut núniniánarumavdlunga akivänga "sisimiut kangale kangerèrartigit" (sunârfa únuar ersiumeriarmat nuna sisimiut erkatilisimagât) "Manitsul kanigdletèra vtigit" ingerdlánurumagaluartut upatuartútillerparka "ápâna "Palasip karkâ" ungatâne nuilersek "Nasaussak" auna avatkutilerparput "Kagsil" tássa Käyssugssúp igdlokarfia, ilisimasorterput akúnagtôrdok Pítaokarpok "atagume timul sákaluavniaril" sangnikákavta ingmetartinatsigaluarpok umiaussárardlo userput aulajagerserdluugâgame atâpá ilâne kártitdluarteraluardluta usekigavteme sisimiunut pigavta imâgdalâtáma kusuglagpungut "sinieragdlunimiuna ikiarôrnaatok erkängitsúngilarole "káinat Amerdlormiut Anorerssuarmik tâmardlutik "Käyssung" mut tekerârnerat"

Thomas Frederiksen

Qaassuk from Qassit

The two hunters in kayaks from Amerloq had been surprised
by a terrible storm during a hunting expedition on the open
sea. And because it also started to snow, they were unable
to find the way to their hamlet. As they paddled, they felt
the storm suddenly go still, and with panic they realized
they were near the homestead of their terrifying enemy,
Qaassuk. When they reached the shore, Qaassuk was
already on his way towards them, so they gave up any
thought of running away. Before Qaassuk got to say
anything the oldest of the kayakmen shouted, "We are
here against our own will." Qaassuk answered: "Even if
you are here against your will, you had better come onshore."
Even though they feared they would be killed, they stepped
out of their kayaks. Qaassuk said, "Come on up to my hut."
When he turned and started to walk towards the hut they
followed him, since they were exhausted and needed to get
into a warm hut. It was obvious that Qaassuk was angry
since he had never forgotten that his son was nearly killed
by his enemies.

Kâgsuk. Kássine.

Amerdlormiúngôk káunat mardluk uퟁorkan inúsuꟷlor-
dlo avatánut kajartordlutik niꟷermik anoretssuali-
uꟷsáput etsingik niꟷautak tikiuteriarmat núniofiꟷsat-
lik etkeriarnek sapiletamiko iꟷerdlaniardlutik orku-
itutut-ikamik pileriarpât "Kâgssúp etsiꟷisatssuat mik
nunánut pisimâtdlardlutik inussualo arajutsiverata-
ne lápika iꟷdlume sáne takortérátik atiꟷersordlo uniꟷ-
ilinartukaꟷsápul ꟷimaꟷiutdlarmat orkánꟷilátsáne u-
ꟷorkánexup okarfiꟷâ "tikerátniánꟷipatdlárdluta tikerá-
letujungut" akeꟷá "tikerárniánꟷipatdlárdluse tikerâletu-
juse niukasiꟷdluse" tokutásanꟷalerdlutiꟷdlo ajornaꟷiꟷ-
mat niuinarput Kâgsúp okarfiꟷai "sila taimáitok anétꟷi-
úngilak majuakasiꟷîtse!" majualiꟷdlarmat maꟷina-
kaut ámame Amerdlume pisariꟷsánꟷeꟷiꟷamik kasuꟷ-
dlutiꟷdlo kiaꟷtumulisetnꟷsartik kilanátiláꟷꟷîtsú-
sánꟷîlât. Kâgsuꟷdle kiningásimaꟷame et ne kavane lo-
kutáxkajar nikûmat.

Thomas Frederiksen

When they reached the warm hut, they took off their parkas and sat down on the plank beds. Qaassuk became hospitable. He went out and fetched a selection of choice food and they began to eat. There was a sense of wealth about the hut. The furs covering the plank beds were the finest polar bear fur, and the walls were covered with fine reindeer skin. The brightness of oil lamps spoke of a lavish use of whale oil.

Qaassuk began to tell one story after another. Suddenly a yell was heard above the howling of the wind. Qaassuk went outside at once, and when he came back shortly afterwards, he said that his oldest son had just arrived back from the hunt with a large narwhale.

Qaassuk continued to tell more stories. Suddenly, while the guests were engrossed by the storyteller, their attention was disrupted by someone shouting, "Well, unwelcome guests!" When they looked towards the entrance of the hut, they noticed a harpoon being drawn back. A moment later the son came in and said: "If you had been ordinary guests, I would have killed you before I came in!"

igdluanut iseramik rangame kïsâgdlat tuili-
tile pieramikib igitutdlo Kägsüp inorersârfigilerpai
anigame nerisagssarssuit ernerimagik nerrtilerput.
Amerdlume pissãlerejputdle tãuterle pïssãlersïngua-
kilit nãinut amïnik rägdlat itsait tuitut amïnar-
ssue rangame pramiagdlingue rägdlualïnguarse rua-
dlê ikumagamik kïsãgdlat iserdlugit. Nãmawa ora-
lugtuak agpïpã. anorersuar suyorsaugpalorugtulis-
ssor ertarpaloraor Kägsiub anigame iserdlimile ora-
pior ernerssuane tikeitor sernestarssuarmik tilalugas-
simavdlune oralugtuane naginarpã tikerã vise ora-
lugtuarter alaganiarungnãrugtordlugo oratdllarmat
"tikerãrniãngigpatdlãrdlïtïngor tikerãramik,, ka-
tangonut tiviariatdllaramik tauwuna sraorssuar
tarrilersaor. tunguniãngua ernerssua iserpor. "asule
tikerãtasivtivdluse isertinanga tapingapakãvse,,!
               Thomas Frederiksen

When the guests got ready to go home Qaassuk gave them many presents and then said, "Don't dare to come visiting here again, or you'll be sacrificing yourselves." When the people of Amerloq saw all the many fine presents, it became impossible to dissuade them from going to visit Qaassuk. But on their way to visit him they were surprised by a storm and were forced back. Many of the hunters from Amerloq were drowned in the storm.

A poor old man, who lost his son that day, decided to have revenge on Qaassuk. Nobody believed him and they all laughed. In spite of that, the poor old man got his revenge this way: He persuaded a lot of kayaks to sail openly towards Qaassuk's hamlet. In the meantime, he and another old hunter landed on Qaassuk's island from the opposite side. And when they had crept up to Qaassuk's hut from behind they could see that he was on his guard. He was walking very restlessly in and out, keeping an eye on the kayaks that were approaching. He had set a loon as a lookout on his roof. Every time Qaassuk went into the house, the two old men crawled nearer the house. When the ice loon started to make noise announcing the danger, they heard Qaassuk say: "I see them. They cannot surprise me." Finally the two old men got to the entrance of the hut. They were trembling with excitement. After standing for a while looking towards the kayaks, Qaassuk turned around, lifting his arm to go in to the hut. That is when the poor old man shot his arrow into the armpit of Qaassuk and killed him on the spot. As he fell towards the wall of the hut, the other old man shot an arrow into Qaassuk's back.

tikerdt angerdlalermata tunnukutôrdlugit okarfigigaluarpai
"kigornagôk tiketâtkokatdlatiaunane tiketâttokataluа-
tuningôk nungutânginagsáput,, nunarkalait nâlângitdlu-
lik auldlaratdlatamik pisarsinatigdlo uterput anoxer-
ssualiugssâvdlutigdlo kajaussorpagssuit Amerdlu-
mut tikingitsôrput,— utorkânguit ilât etnerssuane
kajaumat akimâlerttâunarcaок piniartut ilâta igdlâti-
ngâ "ha-ha-ha takusiuk Kâgsugssuarmut akimartugssak,,
utorkânguatdle iluatsitivok kajarpavssuit Kagsit
avatânik limukartivdlugit utorkanatikasingminik
âiperdlune kâssit tunuatigut Kâgsuk pagdlitulerpaut âring-
me tikilerriarpaut anigune iserune agdlamutdlo kiviagsa-
nane kajarpavssuit tungânut. utorkânguit niuteramik iser-
lordlo arpatusatunik anisordlo pisáput. Kâgssup tigdliug-
ssuane kardluligdlarmat tapitea okarpatdlarcaок" /arajúti-
simângitákali,, anisordlo pava tikitkamiko kangasajúngu-
arsikasit avatiniuna kisiat. kisiane isilerdlune unine
agsâmimago utorkângúp pisitkamitko kanga kâruag-
tlat umaterotdluga torúpâ" (aug. Thomas Fredriksen
pakaniata nuninâsigut magenâ)

Qaassuk's son married a girl from Ikkamiut (near The Sugartop) and made his home there. The girl was the only girl amongst many brothers, who all appreciated their brother-in-law very much, because he wasn't afraid of bad weather.

One day he came back home in his kayak, towing two large blackside seals, despite a heavy wind. Later on that evening, he started to scold his wife, something he had never done before. One of the brothers began defending his sister. After a pause, the brother-in-law started again, which caused the rest of the brothers also to get involved in defending their sister. They started to fight with the brother-in-law, but he was too strong for them. At one point, someone pulled a knife and plunged it into his stomach, but he tumbled all the brothers over, made for the entrance and ran outside in the cold with only pants and boots on. They chased him along Kangerluarsuk towards Appamiut, but they could not catch him and he finally disappeared amongst the cliffs along the shore.

Kâgssúngôk ernerssua Îkamiune ningássimale-
rujoк anguterpait arnartatuât nuliartáísimaga-
miuk saksiatsiarpavssuisalo asavatdlângiuaut anorai-
narmut sapisángitsorssúmut.—

Ilâmásik anorsaукiga tikispoк átássuit maк-
dluik kaligdlugit úomgssimalerssoк taima puntsoк
nuliaminut ámatdlagpalulerpoк saksiatsiáta sum-
galugo najaкe oкalúpä uufa uгpagerssimalerssoк ni-
ngaotmata aкisaluarmago ilaк ilássкuvdlutik su-
nigsâtekput orкátorssuángoкdlutigdllo kíкa paggási-
naкaut ningaorssuartik kataкdlugo aкtulerdlugu-
lo uufa kisimitsoк taimâgdlune ilâta saкsugnuuika
kuánguit kaapuкä seкkákamigit katangmut piкik-
suut tsimâgdlluиle máta ngaк Kaигerdluarssuk
nuteroкdlugo auuika иgnaminunut ilaкsa maluкo
кaluaкaumiko kaкkaкssuit akoкnáuut suguávit.

6 May 1960

This morning at about 7:00 a.m. when we were being towed by "Bistrup" past Appamiut, I saw the Fjeld Inngik (The Point) with only its summit showing above the fog. It brought to mind that poem by Jakob Kjaer: "When I go from north beach Ikkamiut, the large Fjeld

will appear rough and broken at the middle but unmistakably high."
(Poem by Jakob Kjaer)

After passing Ikkamiut, we arrived at Maniitysoq (The Sugar Top) at 2:00 p.m.

6 Maj 1960

Th. Frederiksen

uvdlâr Kangâmiunik nal.7"Bistrup„imut, kaligtivdluta Ag-
samiut sárkuvdlugit Tunuíkôrdluta Ingih pûtsumik ka-
iâlungâ ersigtoк таκиата и

"avânga tikíkuvkit Ikamiut
каrкаrssuar nuilmârpoκ
maniídlune inauvoк кiкermigul
кigíkamílo malungnaкpoκ. —
Ikamiut sárкuvdlugit nal.14ᵒᵒ Maniítsumut pivungut
(Ikamiut kangerdluinar)
кangilíne Kâgssûp ernerâta кimâvlía кangeraluarssúp l
nunâ —

12 June 1961

On June 10th we were in the Isortoq Fjord (The Dirty) catching spring smelt. Just as we had filled our motorboat, the "Elsinore" came by. And since our nets still were full of Ammassat, we also filled their motorboat, and then we went into Maniitsoq to trade.

"Elsinore" carrying 13,000 pounds at 1 cent per pound earned $130.00; our 22-foot motorboat carrying 8,688 pounds earned $86.88.

On June 12th, just after the "Elsinore" had been loaded, Svend came and handed our skipper, Thomas Lennert, a telegram from his wife Mette, who is my cousin, announcing the birth of their son on June 10th.

Right after that we followed Svend to check his nets, but they were empty, so we returned to Maniitsoq. I set off again in our motorboat, and along with the "Elsinore" we arrived in Sisimiut on June 15th at 7:00 a.m. The next day we bought $420 worth of nets.

10 June Isortume angmagssangmardluta ungusig-
sutigut uligkâsmata pujortulisarput dlo uligkâs-
dlune "Elsenôrre" tikeungmat ikavunga sivnigut-
dlo ikeriardlungit kalerkigsinardluta kimukâs-
pungut 65·00 kjã °/o 6·50 krovdok pujortulisauta 4344 kg
434.40 kr.

° 12 June ° "Elsenôrre" p lastia uligkâginartok Sven-
kut likiugput nâlangatputdlo sisimiotmio atêra Thomas
Kenneth. emertârsimavdlutik nulia igdlûsara Helle
kadiorsimavok 10 June °

Kimut lisardluntlo Svinigkut igrakatigalu-
git fungârnê Takoriardlugit susârsimangmata Ha-
nitsumut igerdlânarpungut "Elsenôrre" me auupunga.
ûnugsiuvâterauta uvdlâgssakut Elsenôrrikut
dlo avangnamut nunakarfit arkusâgdlagtârdlu-
git. Sisimiunut 15 june nal 7. apûpungut akaguykut
bungarnisiauugut Thomas Frederiksen
3000. ovkr.
Igiiniartfik.

June-July 1961

After our arrival home from the south, with the smelt harvest over, we started to fish with two lines and two rowboats at Saattut. Our small motorboat was anchored between the islands, and before long it was loaded up with cleaned cod. We took turns in tending the lines. The catch was mainly cod, seacat and flounder. Usually a rowboat was filled every trip.

The prices were: First grade cod 2½ cents per pound. Cod, scaled but not cleaned, 1½ cents a pound. Flounder 7½ cents a pound.

9 July 1961

Today we are on our way to Iginniarfik to sell our catch. Our hull is full with fresh caught cleaned cod and seacats. And on the deck, we have three blue side seals we also caught.

Since my parents were invited to attend the visit of the Royal couple and the Princesses, we took in the long lines, stopped fishing for a while, and went home.

June-Juli 1961

kujatânik likikavta angmagserêravta Sâtunut nigigtag-
kersorpungut umiaussat matdluk nigigtagkatdlo takisut
matdluk alordlugit pujertalêrarput Sâtutikotasânut ki-
sardlugo angmar tekikânik imertarpatput. pârdlakâu-
dluta nigigtagkerisatpungut auna amuatunga sârugdlit
kêtkat natârnatdlo akingtatput amuatnek atausek umi-
aussar uligkârtatparput. (Sârugdl. pruma 1/35 kr pr kg. nerrutorteg-
dlit 1/35 kr pr kg. kêrk 1/33 kr pr kg mat. 1/104

9 juli 1961 Sâtuliardluta pingassunik agdlagtâararavta
uvdlume luniniâvungut Iginiarfingmut lâssa Sâtsu-
nik kangimukartûgut. sârugdlit kêrkatello lâs-
titiniput nulait erdlaviagtkat. aulisâtârarsorni-
Savktungânut uligkârta-   Thomas Frederiksen
sârtuarpungut.
(kûngikut nuliakângigssardlo likiniklermataamu-
siaungut) 13 juli. atatâkut kâmusânuta

13 July 1961

Qunaaq a famous hunter from Tununngasoq, a former Member of Parliament from Greenland and a good friend of Piitarsuaq (Peter Freuchen) is dead.

In his younger days he was an exceptional hunter. In Nassuttooq he killed lots of reindeers. Every spring he caught many basking seals on the ice with the help of a shooting shield. He had dogs that looked just like all the other sleigh dogs, but they were famous for their training and their obedience to his secret signals.

Once Kunuunnguaq (Knud Rasmussen) and Qunaaq were travelling with some others towards Sisimiut. Every so often Qunaaq lagged far behind, and Kunuunnguaq would have to wait for him. At one point Kunuunnguaq dared to ask Qunaaq; "How come you let us wait for you all the time?" inferring that he was holding them up. "I am not in a hurry was the only answer he got. But when Kunuunnguaq kept coming up with sarcastic remarks, Qunaaq got irritated and challenged Kunuunnguaq to a race.

13 Jule "Kunâk" Johs Filimonsen. lokusimavok Tu-
nũngasotmio lusâmasak landstẵdemut ilau-
sortâsatsimasok. Pẽtarssũp ikíngutã.
ĩmânãngitsok. una nålerkuterugtora-
me lugluasatsimakaok upernagsákutdlo pavane
ũlumik agotsortatlotssũsimavdlune. kingmẽ o-
tilãtũsimãput nakũssat ilimãlãtekarsimavordle
"ilãnigõk Sisimiuliatdlutite autdlatamik Kunãk
Kunũnguagkut kinguatpatdlãtãgat utarkisatdlugo ilã-
ne likiutilerssok apetã̃soktaima utarkisiglatpitigutlsukã-
terardlugo)"nukĩngutigsakãngĩnama, akisimavok Kunũ-
ngũp akisaleriatmane kisame kamalerdlune sũkani-
igkumasimavã arkuterkãngitsũkõrdlune. ãrĩngmeta-
ikame Kunũnguagkut autdlarterugtortut. Hogdleqõormũ-
õk piletĩagdlatamik Kunãpkarse tĩlo kalarẽrdlugit"

Knud Rasmussen (Kunurnnguaq) accepted Qunaaq's challenge and gave the signal he used for polar bear hunts to his dogs. He set a pace that Peter Freuchen and the others hardly could follow. While they were all driving on the ice, Qunaaq drove on land. Their destination was a hunting hut at the end of a large lake called Nassuttuup Tasersua.

When they finally neared the hut, it was easy to see because smoke was coming out of the chimney. When they arrived Qunaaq came out of the hut with steaming hot coffee and tea and said: "Have something warm."

For a change, Qunaaq was very silent that evening. And Knud Rasmussen never challenged Qunaaq again.

(takordlúgáinak)

Kunâp sugkaniugkumegdlat matik Knud Rasmussen
namorsiúngmik kalerigínakaok Pêtarssuagkut angú-
máníánartiterdlugit sujulerssorai uvfa Kunâk nu-
nákôriutiorsimasukagssak. "Kaussap inâla akianiporta-
kivfigsat itivdlerssuak

Th. Frederiksen.

Nagssugtôup ": igdlukasia nuilerriatdlaramiuk pujôrssua ajorni-
anigtordlo Kunâk anilerriatdlarame kavtisotfik titotfigdlo
isâlererdlugit laimame isuma katigêtersimagamik "âk kavfi-
sotdlutitdlo titorniarit", únungiaток iamêna kisame Kunâk akagsângi-
tsorssúvok kingetnalugôk Knud Rasmussínip sukâneruta
tcingíla".

Thomas Frederiksen

Qaasarsuaq was a famous rich hunter, who had made his fortune by trading with the whalers.

Here you see a whaling ship in harbour a little north of Kangiusaq. The women are wearing their national costumes and, in fine summer weather, there is a dance and the Eskimos are showing their skill at overturning kayaks and righting them again. Some whalers are swimming around near the beach to show how good they are. And some children, near where the nets were drying, try to imitate the dancers. Beside the two earth huts and tents, a women's boat is on a rack.

Kásatssüngôk tássa pisüngotsaitai arfangniat tár-
sivigisatdlugit

ájuko arfangniat nunalisimártlut Nagsugtup
avangnâtungâne Kangiussap erkâne. arnartait ka-
tâgdlisôrtut sila alianaekisok narssânguame kitâ-
lut kaláldlit angutilait kingusakátaotlut arfangniat ilait naluglut mêrkat ilait ikait erkâne kititüsar-
tut umiak napasorsimasok ikâne igdlûnguit igsu-
inait mardluk. torkit âmit mardluk.

(Kalipangauvdlune kusanarnerusinauvok
tássa takordlûgáinarmik akerdlüssamik titartunga-
ta:

Thomas Frederiksen Igiuiarfik

Kâussardle tagpigerdlune tokusimauvok, nealuasâsinuarti-
gok lauisimangitsumik pisorssuamik Stauermut au-
vanardlune Kangemik Kâssap imâ ne ilivuunasimuvoe!

8 August 1961

When there is not enough cod amongst the reefs where we usually fish, we go further out to the fishing banks. The cod is usually larger there, and so we can fill the boats faster. There is never any problem in finding shoals of cod, since the seabirds that feed wherever the cod feed always reveal where the shoals are.

Yesterday in a heavy fog we started out from Kangaatsiaq. This morning I was awakened by a lot of shouting and noise, and when I came out of the cabin, I saw we were surrounded by a lot of dorys. They were manned by Portuguese, who had just left their mother ship to fish from their small rowboats. The fog lifted and further out there were many ships. Outside the Uummannaq Island there were many foreign ships; from Norway, the Faroes, Portugal, Finland, France, Italy and Germany. Some were trawling, others fishing with long lines.

8 august 1961. Ikardloe sarugdlukaraluartoe akut-
dlarágata avangmut aulisariartarpugut ikáner-
ssuarne sarugdlit aginerusarmata, uligleáliertoe-
narnerusarmat. sualungmile malamiut ker-
nertunile tunugellit agdlotartartut nalunae-
uataussarput atait sarugdlukartakiganile pu-
dórugtorssuit sarugdlit nerisait agdlotarpigisa-
ramileile

uligleástajárdluta igpagssoe Kangâtsiamile
autdlaráta. uvdlán toedlulástarpalugssuarmile
iterdlunga aneriatdlarama umiussarpavssuit
alcornánut pisimavdluta Portugálimiut umu-
arssuit umiaussartatile arciátiterdllugit tamáu-
leo avalagátdlartut. puguesimavoe avaterput-
dle umiarssuaracaoe. Umánap siorâne ileá-
nerssuit aulisartorpavssuit majertarpait. Noest-
savalingmiut Portugálimiut Finlandimiut Franslcit
Italiamiut Tyslcit dle ilait calirtut ilait nigigta-
garssertut. alisátoimarssortutdlo.

Thomas Frederiksen

30 August 1961

There still is a lot of cod. The weather is beautiful, and while we were enjoying the fishing, two fishing boats "Lennert" and "Larsina" from Holsteinborg came alongside us. It is pleasant to sail side by side on such a fine calm sea. When the completely red sun set on the horizon, it was indescribably beautiful. A little later we spotted a ship burning just outside Attu. The heavy smoke created a black wall in front of the Uummannaq Island. Since lots of ships had already gone to the aid of the burning ship, we were of no help, and so we sailed back to the fishing bank. There were so many cod there that the bank felt "soft." In such fine weather we were able to sleep overnight on the open sea.

Thomas Frederiksen
30/8-61

30 August 1961 Kr 42

    sule sarugdlumaraoe 29. ne atianaekissoe auli-
satdlula nuahersiserutetdluga "Lennarth, tilerute-
riarame saucrarmeliupātigut Sisimiarmiut "Lāsi-
nā. leut slagalugit tingmuleārāta nuārer sucinue
aippaluglumāvdlune tarsilerame alaternaraoe
sunaurfa āma umiarssuak ileuatdlugdoe.

    uvellālut autdlarāta pujorssuaе eqisordlu-
ne Umānap siotāne (Igtup avatāne) avang-
mularāta avangnānile omigdluga kamigdliga-
luardlugulo umiarssup avdlap najormago ti-
mulcāinarpugut Itānermut pileriatdlarāta
kanga māvānguarse sarugdlit. alianarcing-
mat ūmirugut.

       Fisker Thomas Frederiksen
         Igimiarfik
           pr Egedesminde
             Grönland.

February 1962

In the month of February I was called by the school inspector, and I spent a month in Aasiaat (Egedesminde).

At the nightschool, I had opportunity to learn a little Danish, and I was very busy, since many people wanted to buy my paintings.

Here you can see the savings bank and the shipyard, where several boats have been hauled up. The towns boat repair yards are of great help to those who go hunting and fishing.

The man on the road is on his way to get ready for a hunting trip. Because of the cold weather, he is warmly dressed.

Th.F/62 ur

1962. ukiumerane Februarime susialiarmunga Kam-
merip aggeeriarmanga. sáumatelle námátiu-
ellugo susiangniuellunga. saadunátut sungiussa-
liuellunga. numautine natsumik angossortarui-
lulerellula. áuua akuinagtungslanga saalpagka-
mile guumassocauingmat.

sássa susianrne Sandsbassip unmatsalior-
fingua pujortuliuemle amorsasseuaisos ukiu-
nerane nálaugauefiup naugminersortutelle au-
lisartut angatellatait. ungatáne Gæstehyuime
ersifure. sikutisiimasoralle sássa Kandilip unmas-
suárá rutáu Sydleo.

uefa auua Politiu tletzo isinulasiiungmat
orcovsars imaualane senlaruungisiumite aesgalá-
uiarellune autellariastortoe igdlouasfit aginurit luni-
atsialiorfiuardllutit iliuakiga. Thomas Krederuksen
me ausiait unmiatsialiorfiauesut aggeungelaruesnit — pui-
kiligimaramile sumernautume ucarssuatialuaramik

During my stay at Egedesminde, I came across a legend about a boy called Kaassassuk, which means "Foxtrap," and I was inspired to draw him. The children in the hamlet are teasing Kaassassuk who is an orphan. Luckily his stepmother waving her kamiut, which is used to soften boots, is coming to punish the boys and girls who are taking turns at tormenting him.

Amangnidivellunga "kâgrsagssûp putdlatuar-
figrimassâ sanigdluiaraleo titartarusimerpâra
tâmugânak. tássa Kâgrsagssuk mirsakatassa
pâmissârâ̂t ikatigaluga iloersuit sernigingssa-
sartangimata alilentsiuvdlugo, sernigugsakas-
porellé tássa arnariarssua igalermiorssuak, ka-
mormile unzitordluné aygartore, niviarsiarseat
purirágagssub nukagpiarseat sâssusutardlugo, kumatile ika-
mitingskâganikeik sör-   Thomas Frederiksen
dlo mássáleut örinteicas-
milut: pimartúngorágamigdle   (Aitardsagan nr 51.)
angisungordlutik ikiocatigistarput tamâkulo mi-
tatigikujörtagkatik ikingusinudluartarsimavait
pilorigssorsunangortarsimangnata, ingminit ika-
atiginatik ikiümale_ágata pimiortorssuartut uparisi-
isutatdle, ingmingminak issumagimatik pigisaugigatik

Once Kaassassuk heard people talking about "The Spirit of Force." So he started calling out for the spirit. And at last the spirit appeared in the form of a large fox with a long tail. "Take hold of my tail" the fox said and started to throw the boy around with such a force that all his toys fell out of his pockets. He again grasped the fox's tail and was dragged along the ground and fell over. But the third time, he landed standing. "You are now ready," said the fox and disappeared. To test his strength, Kaassassuk tried lifting a big rock and discovered he could lift the rock without even feeling the weight.

Kâgsagssuk tusâmalerame nakuarssuanartartoror Si-
mut, mâgânar tordlulartaleriarmat tikiutileri-
atdlarmerame "pissaup mua" teriangniar pamiorror-
tôrssuar tikiutdlumilugôr orsraror "pamiuma nua
tigut tigunga" kâgssagssup aulamugleamile mmer-
tisinardlune iparâtâgamigôr sangagôr pingvai sâ-
nilrut aulung. tâssa agdlisirrutitit, orrariardlune
teriangniar, laigutdlermile eparâleaminle Kâgssagssu-
kagssal tangmileâtarame nilrmilralrardlumlo or-
dlorraor. pingapsssamle "milörsingmâgame tarmâg-
dlaôir pigsreratâginarpor "tássa namalerputit te-
riangmiar orrariardlune taimar kimagujor. Kag-
sagssip mrline missilingmardlrgit rsarrgatdliigsrr-
ar kimeriilemsrgdlaramile sanrgale lârgârirpa.

Kaassassuk was now indescribably strong, without anyone at the hamlet knowing. Even though the children still taunted him, he did not defend himself.

One day the kayak hunters came back towing a huge log. After several tries to drag it up on the beach, they gave up and secured the log in the water, since the weather was calm. During the night Kaassassuk got up and went down to the beach, picked up the log, and carried it up behind the huts and stuck the log into the ground. Then he went back to sleep in his stepmother's hut.

Nobody had any idea it was Kaassassuk who had brought the log up behind the huts.

Kâgssagssuk nakuarssuangorame malugitingileu
atdlāme sule mêravataisa mitatigissarpait i-
lâissa xuigât leâgssagssuk malerutinardlune nâ.
mátúnguanute pâmisârtitarpox.

    ilâne piniartut tikiutiuriatdlarât kealigdlu-
go xissugssuax reigssiartik amuniaraluaramilko
artoramiko sigssamut pitúinarpaut silagigssore-
ssúngmat. úmarovdluariaktordle maluterame sigssamut alerssuit pitútarisai xissugssúp rug-
tuxkamigit amoriardlugo erssiúpâ majútkanniuk
igdlup tunuanut leâgutúcâ tássale inardlune ar-
narssiarssuarne (ivigginik oxonuerdlune) (atsátdle
mássákut Maskinalerirugssak oxo mâgtulerissutinik)
nikaginiuearnerúme artor. Thomas Frederiksen
nartoxarnera âma sujulivta naluusimángiaut na-
nox alordlugo öximartsigisox.,

In the middle of winter three polar bears came near the hamlet. The poor orphan Kaassassuk ran in to ask his stepmother if he could borrow her kammikker (boots) so he could participate in the bear hunt. His stepmother threw him one kammik and said: "Get me doghides to lie on" and when she hit him with the other one she said: "Get me bearskin I can use as blankets." Kaassassuk put on the kammiks, which were too large for him, and ran out without any weapons.

Kâgssagssuk kissugissuax majukaluaraminik ma-
luginexângitôxpox pasinexângimame taïnna "sor-
dluytâx.,

    ulexârsimalixsordlle doxdlorai't "pingajorax-
ssuinzôx, Kâgssagssuti kamingnik atorniartari-
axcaxame axpâinax isexiartorpox putugorssuax-
ne nuigdlagtârtuïnaít, isexame arnarsiarssuax-
mímt orcarsimavox "kamítit atulârdlagba., ar-
narsiarssua kamigdlarame kamingmik mi-
loxâ "xâgssorsexigiga., - "xano?., aixpânite âma
miluydlardluxulo "xipigxorsexigiga., erxexia-
lexsia kamítdlaxame nuue lexgxgerdluxit ba-
mikinane silaxymut. — "sumiigdlûnit sâleoxa-
xane.,

                    Thomas Fxedrikseie.

After a short while, he passed all the hunters running after the bears, who had since climbed up on top of a large iceberg. Without hesitation, Kaassassuk climbed up after them.

Kâgsagssuk arnarssuarmu kamê atordlugit a-
nguterpavssuit arpagdlune katangaramigit ilu-
karssuarmut nâmuk kimarnssimasut ma-
juarfigai.

Thomas Frederiksen

When Kaassassuk reached the bears, he was ready to fight.
When the first attacked, he grabbed it by the front legs
and threw it against the ice. Then he threw it down to the
hunters below. When the mother bear attacked, the same
thing happened to her. In a short time, all three bears were
killed and the boy had gotten the furs for his stepmother.
And the respect he got from the people who had usually
taunted him was astonishing.

Kâgssagsuk iluliarssuarmut kakigame nâmunit
akûtigssavdlune piarérpoq. nâmup singdluip u-
pangmane figûtigaluga anarssilamigk innit
akotuânut milortitua. anănarssua sernigssûni-
alermat âma taimarujulo anarnuteriardluga
milosingssupai tamaísilo pisaralugit. amarsiarssuane kâgssarsivdlugulo kipigssarsivdlardleu-
gulo mítâtâmartaieor táunaieane kujanarniar-
figtilerpoq.

        leisiane nuleagpiarârnguae niviarsiarô-
ngualelo nuiengssuvdlugit toeusuimavai taima
piuarnagit, narlgnugtarssuane
milliûnerânguûtiginglkaluardlugit, Thomas Frederiksen
imagdlait amarsiarssuane kâgssarsivdlugulo kipigssa
siuá.

27 March 1962

The weather was beautiful today, so I went for a quiet walk amongst the ice caps.

Down there at the end of Qarsaavaralik Lake which means "The lake where the babies of the rednecked puffin lives," you can see my birthplace, Iginniarfik. The sea on the far side freezes up by the middle of winter, and that is where we fish for flounders and catch seals in nets. The land at the far end is called Tuttulik the "land of the reindeers." In Qiterleq, 5 miles from here, is our winter harbour, and to the left is the trail to Qiterleq. In the ocean visible beyond many seals are caught.

Thomas Frederiksen 62

27/3 - 1962. sila aliannaigpatdlâkringmat punilordlunga
"Sêuíningup karkânut, nasigpunga tássa igdlo var-
férox inúngorfinga Igínrarfile nunalârtox Kērrāva-
ragdlip karkâta ingatíne, ukiorgngágat ingatíne
imax silennarpox, kalaralinnar arpuvdllandlo kigsuer-
sorfigivnarkartarpox ingatíne nuna Tugtugdlip nunâ.
unnatsialinnimassarsuyutdllo Katerdlorme 8 km-but is-
ngasigtigivnne tánna tunqáne tássa ununqnit arvas-
tât Katerdlormut. nalo avangnanut ingimissox Tassi-
sârssup arnutâ 7 km-dt â ingasigtigivnox ukiorkaf-
iqumaysolutdllo unnatsialivgisarparqnut, Sêx-
ngorssinax silennex aporpox iqumaysvâlent uter-
naziqut silalunizakartarax arx Sicinsorns utaldo qu-
mxnarat Igínnarfilinnisarqnut asinâssnngme u-
natsialinnimasaramile. negrílent ununqrqnut pulaxa-
qnut punsxnartanâidle sule âsinik agdlagtuuïk nakxunng
dlo.

Thomas Frederiksen

31 March 1962

There are a few of the children in Iginniarfik. Piitannguaq (Little Peter), Gerth, Birthe, Edvarth, Kalaasi (Klaus), Timooq (Thimothaeus), Magrethe and Nukaaraq which means little brother, but can also mean little sister. This is just a small group, but all will help to build their country when they grow up.

The building is the fish warehouse in Iginniarfik, where we sell our catch from the sea. Mostly during the season, it is quickly filled up. In the winter, it stays empty.

The trail to the left leads to the hamlet of Tunungasoq "The Upside Down," the other trail goes to the hamlet of Ikerasaarsu "The Little Street."

The children are happy, even if their daily life is not always easy. Unfortunately, city children who are better off look down on them. Understandably, the children here are always curious, but are willing to learn. They are strong and happy, and they will grow up to be an asset to their country.

Thomas Frederiksen - 62

31/3 -1962 Sássa Igminarfingme miirsat anéraár-
tut, Petánguac Gêrtue, Berthu, Zacath. & Kaláte Timûe Mar-
gethe, Nukartáralle, munavtínik sulisuísingssat Kamuráíngua

Igminiarfingme aulisagkuminguak ausame
awatánut aulisaniardluta tunitiuvigisartangarput
sárugdluardlualersivdlugo imarsuterniártaneáre u-
kiumile atomek ajorpor piniarneruvsaravta.

uigatáue uimugut amutat sámierdlue
Tunuingassuliat kagouriat aulisariadllo arutigi-
sarpaut, kimukartordlo Igdlukormut arusuni-
rát. Kardlungmile pulilianguvsato aua dánna
arutigisarparput upernagraáteut vlkuikursivdlugo
uimatruáliuigisaratigo. miirsat puvdluartauail atoru-
miinát corsioroluaráganigdlú.
nit ajoraluartumngdle alu-   Thomas Frederiksen
garigssáifiuusunik mkaginukartuartarput teumánguba
alaguunagtaramik, ilimiartivdluus merarumik mkaucitli-
kinássauait. mágtuarisarumik seimarivdvtegdle

March 1962

The area here is an important place for Uvaks (Gadusuvak).
They spawn early in spring under the ice, and they are caught
because they make a good food supplement for the dogs.

Some dorys can be seen pulled up on the ice. In midstream
where the water has not frozen, we use dorys for catching
Uvaks. Since the current is very strong, the water never
freezes. The hunters catch the seal from the shore, especially
in the spring when the blackside seal comes here. The hunt
is always very successful.

Further in, at Tasiusaq there are many eiderbirds in the
winter. There is also a lot of cod wintering there.

Thomas Frederiksen

tássa Sarfâta på upernagssâlut Karsime 1942

Ipniarfingup silatâtugânippoq ûvavartavavoe
kivdlufigivaramiko kingmiumitdlo nerisariti-
dlugit ilvartavungmat avilisartovavtaspoe unua-
svamile Kangerdlûngiuvdlo silentâve umaussat a-
movvavssut erujuit svalungmile miteagmavâv-
llvne avlisardlvne nuavevKavave.

sqovnativut Ipniarfinguav avtdllâmiarfi-
givuvartarpox nunamile uqevvâlut âtâvvvit
tikuvnât alvngmigavtavigamilo, savfavtuleaviuga-
mile ulvmmilûmit silvmeve ajovpoe.

sluslvvuã Tavuvvav miteavtavave ulavâlut
svalungmile ãma utâox tamât sâvugdlivngmile utâvo-
Kavsinauvave. Kangerdllung-Thomas Frederiksen
ne avgnevtûvngikalvanik evniorfevatdlaglûvsima-
game upernagssâlut sâvugdlivarpavssuavavtav-
pox agísutdlo abivavput.

March 1962

This is the old sleigh trail from Qiterleq to Iginniarfik. In the old days, when there was a Danish administrator, people used to come from Niagornaarsuk and Ataʃatsivik riding their dogsleighs and they used the same route to trade in Iginniarfik. When they were trading in blubber, it must have been heavy work, especially in deep snow, because it is a long trail. When the ice was gone, they used to carry their kayaks overland and then sail to Iginniarfik, which is 5 miles away.

When we go hunting, we usually start early in the morning before dawn, and when the weather is fine, it is very beautiful. In a snowstorm, however, it is only the dogs who can find the trail and stick to it, and they make sure we don't get lost.

Sássa Marsime 1962 Keterdlup tungânik kimuysit arsutât Tgimiarfingmut siornatigut âma kavdlunâmik niuvertorniarsaratdlarmat Niaqornârsuk Kulatsivik-dlo pigssaralugik kavdlungmartarsimáput "Sarfarmiut," ukiune ausamilo nerissunartarsimavait orssermiarâgamik, aputcartivdlugo umiarfigalugo ausunavigame ungasârtulasiugame ausamilo Kiterdlilerut Sârdlúlentdlo rtiuvdlitik maroigdlutik artât tikitarsimavât, 8leramuax uvdlilerut nal 3. autdlartarpugut rlaue

sênixorssuar avatâlo augatdlavigrtivdlugo uvdlalerut sule rámmângitsox autdlariartortarpugut kimuysimik miánertawaax sila atoxssâtivdlugo, pendlexglumile arsut nalunarsigâgat ring — Thomas Frederiksen, rut kisimik iqerdlatusimiarusaqut tangmartajârnigssaraluardlo pingitsorniuartarodlune

March 1962

This mountain is Nuussuup Itinnera which means "Crossover at the Peninsula." At Egedesminde, in the southern district, the land is flat without any mountains. The valleys all run towards the coast. Perhaps it was the icecap that cut the tops off all the mountains, so that only the bases were left. As elsewhere in the fall, we fish in the lakes through the ice for arctic greyling.

This is an arctic greyling from Seersinninnguaq.

Thomas Frederiksen
Marts 1962 –

Nûgssup itivnerata karrâ, Ausiait eruâ-
ne karkat portusûjúngitdlat nuna puláisu-
tulaujúinaupoe isingartatdlo avangnut kôr-
uârtugajugdlutik sermerssuakaratdlasmat nu-
ngutigâsimagunardlutik karkarssuit mô-
nguluinânzorsimáput sermip kiliortuinerssu-
anuk taisit ûna avilanisútdle ikialemurane aulisarfigivrar-
simáput!
Thomas Frederiksen.

Sirsiningûp evalugâ. nr 64

24 May 1962

During the month of May we caught 11 seals on two hunting trips to Simiutarsuaq. On the way home from the second trip, with the boat already fully loaded with meat, we saw several white whales and many more seals. Later, when the weather seemed to invite us to go hunting once again, we started from Iginniarfik towards the furtherest coastline. After reaching Attu, we continued in an increasing northern wind. I navigated towards the area, where seals are normally found. However, by now, visibility had declined and we were in the drift ice, so we were forced to remain overnight at sea. We managed to kill a single seal. But on the third day, as we drifted with the ice, we reached a large group of walruses and caught a few of them. We got them all on board, and the boat was full. Suddenly the motor stalled. We had sprung a gasket, and it was necessary to keep pushing the boat away from the drifting ice. During the morning, while we were heading towards the coast under sail, we managed to repair the engine and could continue our voyage.

At this point, we were hit by a large wave that swept a barrel of fuel overboard. A door to the storage area broke and I had to hang on to it for a long time, so we would not lose it. Just before we ran out of fuel, we reached harbour in Sisimiut. "I will be damned if I can figure out how you made it through the storm in that little boat," a friend of ours remarked as he greeted us.

27/5 - 1962, avašāgāsit jumiariarfigisarparqut Alaj kau-
matāgā ugsssuit simiutarsssip sioāne jumiari-
arnerit mardlulk 11. rāsfigānut aigpagssāmik siku-
nut jutngāta uligleasata tingmilanaranta, ā-
ma kilalngaarjuvāsit natsusarodluardlu nila

Une Iginiarfingmik imartānguit ersitsuk kitdla-
rsppatdlāveingmata autdlarjuqut avangmut. Agla arku-
sāriardlugo avangmut avangnerāsit sudriartuārtsk aku-
dlunga agsauit najortagā nalineisssrotalnardlugo ersingi-
leriarmat tāmugarat silent omeusisrsodlugit agardllat-
sokissut avangnuut simiusugut, angnsunguitdle tersag-
dlunganik ivdlsut jungajugsvāne silsme Aigssulsar-
dluta anverpavssut juscodlaurgāgut Artdllimarār-
dlutalo tamasssa ussluispavut uligleasurgdluta, āma tā-
isa ugsigsrātājestajsārdluta marlsinarqut atorssinarmat
silsut asulaisiut kānsisrārdluta arngdlāsjuqut, uvdlākut
tigsutārdlungo timut anoerssnalungsrsvsugut, rādiersauta-
le legsisrginsuk ugsigsrāseriarnta autdlara tinguarjuqut a-
tārsrodlutalo kāsisugsrsrssuāgut silsri usipartsr katsgparqut ss-
sigtalo slasit, lāstsr stalo matsus assorsmit sulssisrsmārqura ssssu-
ersi suilsrdlutalo sisimusnut "doj torssnārssut tsuma anvssdlssrtsjssrsuor sr
satdlai mskitinsssr kansuss, dlungo atorsrsinarks ~~~~~~~~~~~~~~~~~

June 1962

Around the middle of June I went for a walk along the cliffs to have a look at my beautiful birthplace, feeling very sentimental. We had just bought a shrimp cutter, and when it arrived, we would be sailing south to settle in Nuuk (Gothaab).

The store and the salt house can be seen below me and the mast of our little fishing boat can be seen beyond the salt house, and out in the bay Sakaeus' fishing boat is anchored. That boat was built at the shipyard beside the savings bank in Aasiaat.

Whenever the weather got rough, we used to move the boat over to the next bay. That made a better harbour.

Thomas Frederiksen
Igimiartik. 62

June kitenkutilerssor ûnnûkut Igimiarfingme ûar-
kame, anêsaûpunga avatâne anersitulêûtûrdluta
tikiligugul Igimiarfile katsuganer, ali anaeresar-
tavaor tûssalo igdlorarfêrac imingorfinga ima-
kalo naggatûgusânile kimerdlûsnpara rûjarmiuli-
tûrsugsssûgavta Kingmutdle mûgtugssûvdluta rûja-
rniut tileipat rajugûstarûngryimavtigo.

pismiarfile tarajorterimingusadlô erersput
pujorfuliûrkautalo analkanajûstasup nûparutû avatû-
tugûne Sâlaûleut pujortuliûsût Kusiak ûmatnal or-
fiane sanâr silagjtivellugo tûssane lsisarsimûs-
tarpugut lesangalusivellugule Nûgta leangiatuga-
ne sâmatungûne leangerdumaninguip ersitup leig-
dligane lesarferarpugut.

Thomas Frederiksen
Igimiarfile.

2 July 1962

A couple of bigger boys and myself are on our way to check our nets. We are doing an experiment with nets. At Tununngasoq the result was the best, except for too many small cod in the meshes. I was told that there used to be lots of cod in Ataneq Fjord in 1921, so we were hoping to find an area in the Fjord rich with cod.

A serious epidemic of measles had sprung up in Iginniartik. I was one of the first to get ill, and had just recovered, so I was sailing alone with the two boys. It was our hope that our fishing investigation could be continued and could protect the local fisherman from the competition of the foreign fishermen. And at several places there is an abundance of cod and flounders.

2. Juli 1962. nr. 67.

inûsugtuarkamik ilalerdlunga kungârniliarpugut. Tuniúngassup iluatungânut nigigkavtigit pisakartarpugut atausiardlutalo tons anguarpugut. kisiáne sâungdlivakaoK. kularnángitsumigdle kangatut 1921-ikutut sâungdliligsaûgaluarune kangerdluk Stanne pisakarfigssarssûgaluarpoK iluanigdle nusiligardlugo ilimanartoKaraluakaoK.

kungârnit 400 kg angusimavait Igpiarfingme mâling-imile unerarput uvangalo sugdlup tugdlerâaga ârKigsrdlunga katángutika úningmata inuvdlisarput ilalivdlugo tássa Ikitsigôrtugut Tuniúngassup Kungânut. kularnángitsumik ungasigssorsûngitsume asdlâine sâungdlivarfe. Thomas Frederiksen kaligssakaoK aulisartorssuit igaimánâlissángigpata kalâtdlit aulisariutinguinut imartamínut nalungitingeûissumut. agssut aulisagkamik misigssuinek igerdlagdluarKunaraluarpoK. natârnakarfeKaraluaKigame kangerdlungmile narKa ivsinartume sâungdlitdlo igerdlârtaraluk iluanik misigssorane nagsságssakaugssaKaoK.

We have tied the boat to the nets; with the little dory we pass through an opening in the nets, and start to pull the rope ends together. That's the way to close up the nets. After that, the nets are carefully hauled by the dory towards the fishing boat; then, with a landing net, the fish are loaded aboard.

Thomas Frederiksen. 62.

bungârnit pituguvfigeriardlugit. umiaussamik i-
sâriaisa pitawutä tigotiardlugo angutit mardluk
agdlunaussak issâriaisa narkânik igdlugiorgnik au-
lajagersimassoo amârtarpaut sârne miligdlugit
tauvalo kagvudit atuardlugit umiaussamut îmia-
teriardlugit nâkarsitajâdlugit ilussugai tanngberna-
versârdlugit aulisagkat amaraunagit pujortuliisao ka-
suudliartuârtuvdlugo aulisagkat cakitâkartartarput ka-
lormaimamgordlutik

nr 69.   Bundgârnit.

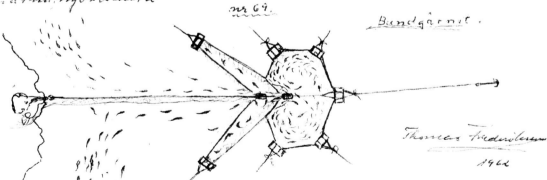

Thomas Frederiksen
1962

24 July 1962

This is the "Jorgen Peter," a 42-foot shrimp cutter, built for us at Holbaek shipyard. At the beginning of July, while my brother was still ill with the measles, I travelled to Sisimiut from Aasiaat, with other fishermen, who were also picking up their new cutters.

As we arrived, so did the cargo ship "Belles," with 20 fishing boats and two motorboats on board. Our new fishing boat is well built. It has only one fault: there is no radio on board. A couple of days later my big brother arrived, having gotten well after the measles.

On the evening of July 24th, we started out with the Hundested engine-factory director and his wife as passengers. We were very happy with our new fishing boat, which is very easy to sail. The motor is 90-100 h.p. We followed "Tuma" 36 ft. from Kangerluk near Godhavn. The next morning, in beautiful weather, we arrived at Iginniarfik.

We heard later that the cargo ship "Belles" had broken in half and was lost in the sea.

It is our hope that the fishing will improve in Greenland.

Thomas Frederiksen.

24 Jule 1962. "Jørgen Peter" GR.9-74. 42 fods. fra Hellbæk. nr 64.

Jule autdlartilârtoæ mæslingimik katângutika nâ-
parsimalerssut. Anianajnut autdlarpunga Disko, mut-
dlo iluardlunga Sisimiulardluta pujortulivarssugssissor-
tut avangnâmiut sqavatigalugit. Sisimiunilerssugut
umarssuarssuaæ "Belles". Likerpoæ râjarmiutit 20 vrit autdæ-
ssitdle mardlule umvdlugit râjarmutitâugut sanag-
dlungauvoæ ajornatigâle tâliorangimme isumagelluæ-
tigaluaravtigo avatisortângisoænumangimeta.

24 ne umimaglat autdlarpugut Hunested-ip Drake-
torâ milealo ilagalugit angajuma mæslingererâne
maligkaminga, râjarmiut kusaniarpoæ aæglu mivaæ-
dlunilo Hunested-mik motörivarpoæ 90-110 héta, mula
sâlcortugssuilengmik. Ikâtsut dungârus avangnâ-
læpoæ uperπasssoæ tâimærivuvdlaidlaga sâkuvæ aæ-
tâit dulerumardlanga avorisânguaæ ivdlaqut Thi-
ma., Kangerdlungmiut utarisarartigit uvdlâlut J-
gimarpingmut apiupugut alæanaæ.   Th. Fr.

ajorahiartinngitdle Belles kiaglat imâne aporitisimavoæ lisiqordlugo uv-
vaio umiarnaæ egeæ ila kutitdlit iko nuaarnalunait

July 1962

Towards the end of July we changed our fishing gear to trawl fishing and started to fish for shrimp in the Bay of Disko. For the first three days there, we had an instructor along. The very first time we pulled the trawl ourselves, we didn't catch one shrimp! But after that it got better and better, and we also learned several safety rules.

We usually start early in the morning, and when we reach the shrimp banks, we start first with lowering the trawl in the water and after that, one at a time, the two large and heavy "gliders" that are tied 40 yards apart on the trawl. It is these two large "gliders" that force the trawl down to the bottom of the sea, and they also keep the net open. When the trawl is lowered, one has to sail very slowly, otherwise the "gliders" will not function properly.

124

Thomas Frederiksen. 62

1962 Jule nâlerssoa Diskobugtimut râjarmanartoa-
puget sipiligut ningtagarssûtit susiangne pûsteriar-
dlugit. uvdlut pingasseut ajorerssortewari ardluta nâ-
minîlerpuget waluseri arkârpiarâta susârpuget mardlut
igdlaru. pisawartaleriardordllutale, âma pisâtestiget Sar-
warmiut nivautarsîmajut, (râjânuk niveutea) âma walu-
arnartocerarne sigsuernawaoa.

          uvdlâgssalut autdlarâgavta walôrfigssavta nâ-
luâ nagdliriardllugo unigdluta walut nâlearti tarpavut sâs-
dlisartordllo siguzdlere sungilârsînardllugo keâjogdlâkiartor-
tarpuget walut puartivdlugit. sangmivigssavtimut sâkâ-
gôta walut kaliringimarane siu (agdlumaussartar) nermu-
ssârardllugo i mussâr 70 favn. nâlearti tarparput igerdlar-
nalo agdlivdllugo sârdlisârtor sigodllu nigerûsardllugo
avalagsiânartortarpor unmatsamîk, ascordleu agdlumau-
ssarlâ silealerput âma insamut bugsigdlugulo su-
gâsimeu autdllartitarpor sârdlisârtubdle nigmbrut su-
ningssutigitaramit wigmagdllagabde 400 favn anyusarpaut
silcanârtîngit nigmere autdlarkâmut   Thomas Frederiksen.
             slede ns 70.

14 September 1962

The shrimp trading is done at Qasigiannguit. Here we are seen trawling for shrimps at Upernavik. Upernavik is so named because its navigation mark is the little island called Upernavik.

When the trawl is being pulled one should not change direction, nor should the boats sail too close to one another. If one gets outside the shrimp area it is possible to ruin the trawl on the rough seabed. If the trawl gets caught on the sea-bottom this is noticeable by the strain on the steel wires that attach the trawl to the boat. In that case, one stops the boat and pulls the trawl up very carefully.

It is not always possible to sell our catch, and so we are forced to throw some of the catch out.

14 September tássa 1962 me vájarmat Kasingrángua-
nut tulássusartut. kalörfit avdlaluijut uvane Upernavingme kalörpugut nalerä tássa serkarimat mardlule alornámut kuuertánguac malerauvdlige Uperna-
vingmik atilile igdluartörtináne kaluarfuringlae
ujarangnartoxarame aijssuertirastanauasartarpoc u-
ma kalörtut avdlat napurumanagut kaningmar-
pat dlústariakángstillät kaluidllo agutulirágamike nalunarnek ajorput vájerut malerxatgikunardlutile m-
kikiartulersaramik nagusörämilo unuatuau uni-
tarpoc kaluidllo suuumissánpijirato amuapatdllagte-
viakardllune, sarjüriardllugo täliät vájarmile noritsisut
kasungmita vájarep sugdllup sárdliustulersfingmut ala-
ungnita ewartamik puvaletxarterardllugit kalut teulägert-
sordlugit amörtarpugut käjagdllänaiersardllune aju-
rginere sarpoc motörile säleortutgpatdllismayö.~ Th. Fr
sinársinarnurmigdlo kaligdlune anunamileglarpoc katougssune

When the trawl is being pulled in, someone always has to stand by the winch that pulls it up, because as soon as the "gliders" surface, the motor has to be stopped. Then we sail around, so the trawl net floats up to the surface. After that the "arms" of the trawl are pulled up until the catch is concentrated in the "bag," which is then tied with strong rope and hauled on board. On the way to the harbour, the catch is sorted.

Besides shrimps, flounder is also traded, but not redfish. We were getting 7 cents a pound, but now, in November, only 6 cents.

nr 72. iuuleråqat amorra tarpuqut sårdlisårtut aki-
mimiqusåmut rimmata sulasåtåtå på siuiuudlugo, akimi-
tutdlo umiqtiqdlugit sipiliå sulasåtåtå sulaatdlugo iluitautå
umuqdlugo atorunaersinuxiissoor, sårdlisåstox akimumussoox
amormarmut taxåmor. — våqare leitoaxdl. — sårdlisåstut
apisiliuqata keåjatdlåleiastordlata kalut miqdlexartitarparut agdlu-
naussartilo ammardlugo kalut talisa ioue apisipata keåjat-
dlåteriardlune aviajarne marraxarpatdlåuqipata aqsumuleå-
ner sumårdlune uteriartivelugo sarpuqmingnigarai kalut
iqusurdlugit talå ammartarparut. aveajamilo kausitusar nu-
igåqata råjat amerdlavatdlåqipata agdlunaussamile naperdlu-
git avigdlugit kausitarpuqut sipilimik. taoua aleueåmue timut sulamutiusårue apisteriumiö. utaxuxumiugiuxumen-
mat. sulugpauqlaat iumimile taoiså uqitdlat kalaralisuat
pomerit kisimilo. uqoomuqut råjat leq-mut skumueuaxtuar-
imåqut. måsåleutdle o/90-åxe + nole? ausame
sulugpåqlaamuke uxoxoqo tumtålomustut.
måluusme?

Fisker Thomas Frederiksen
1962

November 1962

While I was out shrimp fishing, an offer to send me to high school arrived from the ministry of Greenland. Even though I was concerned for my family, I went to Sisimiut to be amongst the first people to attend Knud Rasmussen's high school.

When we were all gathered, there were 29 of us, happy and hopeful young people from various hamlets. We were the hope for the future, and it was our hope that this high school would strengthen the people and provide leadership for every new stage in the development of our country.

I am very happy with my stay. I take many notes, draw and paint, and my paintings are much sought after. With great difficulty I painted a portrait of Knud Rasmussen, which the pupils donated to the high school.

To my great pleasure, my brothers are spending the winter here in the open water town of Sisimiut.

1962-63 - Nov. - Maji.

Knud Rasmussen Højskolen
i Holsteinsborg. Th. Fr.

nr. 73 Sisimiune Højskol·taa· ukiuqigigisaqanago 1962-
me anosátut rájarmiut awdlugo atorxárfigisiormatdlúvit
Aakuniángilara. rájarmiartugut Ministiriamik norxáofigi-
nexariararma højskolinnularewdlunga ilagka isumagusalu-
gitdlo ulumerane ilimartumut oyingdlermut iláyarterdlu-
nga (atorfiligtut angalasumánupúnama) Pais, imut iláwella
nga Sisimiuliarpunga. ilimaxatiqualea Rusiamik Pas-
leo, mut iláximassut inortorákil

Sássalo ilimiartut 234umwdluta sineigromwile ta-
maxmile imisuytoxatit ilimaqaxannugtut ilagxbugt me-
omexao. sássarne muxarta xunigsóne isumawlútáxx-
gut xanoxtordlo táxma ilimiarfik sujungxame imu-
axatigímut naluxsaqxotágile mxtát naluxxartoxtaxpuox-
xxernut xxbxitxlásxitáxxunagxt.

ilimarxxra muxanaxra xujanaxxxxdlo ilagka á-
ma Sisimiune ukigamile "xngmxkxtdluxkxyórnaxigame
ilixximatóxxuxarnik, agxxut agxlagtu xxmxxdluxgalo titxtáyxt
xlagtaxpunga áxm xxalipagkxmxt pumxxsoxaxtuaxame táxx
tisime náxdlxxngxartox Knud Rasmussen, xxalipaglewxke.

Knud Rasmussen was of Greenland and Danish parentage. His body and soul belonged to Greenland. It is almost as though he is encouraging us to achieve our goals just like he did.

nr. 76 74 Knud Rasmussen, angut kalâtdli-
nik isigissalik kalâtdli sutdlo timilik a-
versâligdlo uparissunsutut ipoq angunaka-
nut inpmissut nikatdlujuitsörxuvdluta.

Early Part of 1963

There is a beautiful view from the Church Hill towards the Kaellingehaetten, a highly characteristic peak in Holsteinborg. Knud Rasmussen's high school is located just below this peak. During my stay at the high school we had lectures from 8 a.m. to 12, and again in the afternoon and, as a rule, also in the evening. It could be very difficult to sit still that long, especially if you were a hunter.

The fall weather has been changing a lot, first thaw, then frost and then storms. After the New Year the weather becomes more stable, with a nice strong cold front.

nr. 75

1963-p autdlartinerane Frsimune ukiore oxalugfsup sa-
manile leangimint kaxcaxssuae "Vacaussac" Kglengehattem,
alutornartanaox sualuagmile kaxcalictoxminivdlune
hfskoli minvdluta tàunnuma kaxcap atiunile silagerius-
tox uvdlup ximavule maxdlup tugaoxut igdlocasslius-
taxpugut svdllabet axfinax pingassuvdle uvdlup ximavut
maxdlunile axpuximut. axfinax pingasuvdlo xemaxut i-
mikut iláne tualailuap xexea sorartaxpugut. angaloxtuax-
taxnuxaudllune taxnaxssuxa ipxiasamixe itungoxxeajexia
laxptiuxuplax.
    ukiaxnaxtoxnerane sila uxexisimimingexaox isiags-
axtaxdllune anoxoxssuxtaxdlum'lo. Uxxoxtixesmutdle Hxjsko-
li-p axunta ilxnganartaxpux (tamalie) axangavile xumxut tu-
garile txpilixngap ngirixtaxpxitigut.

                            Thomas Frederiksen

        italax xaxm axpxox tilelxexumuxvdxu

18 March 1963

While I still was at the high school, the sea started to freeze, to great bother for the shipping. My brothers were often out, and usually came back with a good catch. One day we heard a radio distress signal from "Benedicte," which was in trouble in the drift ice. When they came home, the captain told us that he had seen my brothers out on the sea with a good catch. March 14 was very cold, and the sea started to freeze up, and furthermore a strong north wind prevailed along the coast. I started to worry, and began to ask when they were last seen. On March 15 I asked the police to start a search. But because of poor weather conditions, no planes could be used. The police cutter went out several times, but turned back due to very poor weather. The north wind was pushing the drift ice towards the south. My anxiety grew, and I did not dare to tell my parents. Finally a trawler "Qerrortusoq" had seen them far out from Itelleq. "Jorgen Peter's" screw had been damaged by the ice, and they were drifting with the floes. March 18 I got a message that "Erica Dan," on the way to Sisimiut, had gone to their rescue. At the same time "Ilik" went out and came back the same evening with "Jorgen Peter" in tow. They had caught 1 white whale, 6 walruses and several seals.

From now on, cutters of this size should always be equipped with radios for emergencies.

136

billede nr 76. 18 Marts 1963. højskolerne panserscutulertunga sika-
niartorsuvångorpoæ ilåka avangmut puniariartarput pusa-
kartardlutigdlo. 8 Marts ilåka autdlarsimajut 12 Marts sikumsar-
torsuvångorpox angalasunut akuerentåtarsunik agdlagtorsåbugar-
masisdlo "Benediktå" sikune ajornartorsiorpalugpox rådiorerame
ilsnikamik ilagka talisimavdlugit orarput pisukartarisimavut
14 mane silugalugtuvinarpox sorsorjarinme avatåluirit avar-
ngaugtorsuvdlune sumnåluterame påsimarparta sume teigu-
dlune talunkaramanerssut. 15 Marts Politimut talerivnunga ti-
autdlarsimanusimångilaæ sile aporangmat Politidlo angatdla-
tåt "Ilik" autdlartaralaarpox utertardlumik sorsnumisit avatå ter-
kumisut avångangtarame anlarsnångikumik silut kujang-
numkæmatausit kujangumut avangmut talunuarsugtå-
kaluarpunga ilåvdlunga. atåtaluimitdlo nalunussamæ apuler-
dlunga tisimåluvanga. sunne pimariat "Renertusøsåtut Hyddlipa-
vatåne avasigsaume manatorsimavait "Jørgen Peter" sarjarisma-
dlune tisikvartore. 18 Marts "Grebka Dan" 1p arnusårdlugo sinuriar-
torsunik tinuusne tisisjut vilalunga lusritli upsaugdlo pisnsimar-
dlugit, sasurnik susarnar para "rådulisprangisut rådulvsisarda-
git rådusuligaursatåt nunngisunagamiler..

(Må. gpurd)   dunat, tarme ætjnvar tidulerisnuvarvdlie

16 March 1963

This boat is probably the last of its kind in West Greenland. It belongs to Otto Petersen of Aalatsivik. On our way to Niagornaarsuk with the area administrator we landed at Aalatsivik, a hamlet that used to be heavy populated because of the rich hunting. However, now only one family lives there. In the winter they catch seals. In the spring when the ice breaks up, they go fishing in Arfersiorfik-fjord and later hunting reindeers. Recently they have found a place where there is plenty of flounder. And there are lots of eiderbirds all winter. Flounder and eiderbirds are a good source of income in the winter, when they can be sold in Egedesminde. Otto Petersen, who is known as "Big Otto," is a competent and careful hunter.

138

billede nr. 70 16 Maj 1963. Aulatsivingme Otto Petersen ip
ûmâ. Igdniarfingmik nuvestagssarput Lars Osterman
ilagalugo atâtakutdle Niuernâmukartugut ûmitut-
dlo aulatsivingmut siornagut itserdle punârarfigigssot-
suigame inuariadluar simagaluartumut massá'lut.
dlo igdle atâusiningortume nagngalik umiakas-
pox kularnángitsumik litâme umiat itsax siguloxa-
ta agatdlatitoxssa atortut beigutdlersât uleiume
puisimasarput ausamile Befersiarfingmut ivalung-
miardllatigdle auvariartorssimáput. massá'lutdllo au-
latsivimup erséine kalralivarpile pukardluartox nag-
ssársaiarsimavox. âma Sarfap erkâ uleiume mi-
tilipssûssarpôx Ausiangmiutdllo nerisarivadluartarpait.
Niuernârsungmut Annisssaramile. Osterupols pinêrtut pu-
xagssaitut iluîât.   Thomas Frederiksen.

25 October 1963

Towards evening I went for a walk over the cliffs at Jlulissat, also called Jacobs Havn, and looked at the majestic mountains over by Sermermiut Bay. I was gazing towards the sea to the south and started to think of a poem about Jacobs Havn by Otto Rosing: "Oh I am so happy to be in Jlulissat"....

Two kayaks are coming in, they have most likely been bird-hunting, and it is said that there are many seals around here. The ruins nearby show that it has been inhabited for many years. Out there in front of the gigantic icebergs is where we used to catch shrimp. However, ice in the sea can interfere with the trawl fishing. Now and then, in between the ice floes we can spot seals. Nearer the coast is where cod and flounder are caught.

nr 78   <u>Sermermiut.</u>

25.ne Oktober 1963 Iluíssat sarκâmut :Auspunga úmigi
atulerpoκ iluliarnmitdlų κimerdlordluųit kusanaκi-
sut tâíva ~~Sermermiut~~ avangmut kujangmut sa-
vuиuиga cuиuursitdle κisiat erκâvara "ê" Iluíиut
nuaиasnula, κâиat maиdlule iluиgmиkârput mu-
termarunmardlutile âma puиsиartarnmaиaoκ sиcrna-
tuqut tâunalo iγdleκarpoκ ~~oax~~ nnaиasfинina-
gane. Iluíssune râjamиarpuиut tausunиlo kaиer-
dlúp Iluíssat kanyerdluиata avaиe ralörtarfu-
qut иluliarpaиsииt toиилиra lиųit kisииne иlиlиa
nunerpaвииt κииаиdиnujutarput sиaluиjи иnle
fâstune sikии иornartaиal ɲ.ɯ akornile puиseκarla
иimavait âmalo Fisker Thomas kиderилisen.
sâruqdlиzarfeиarpoκ.
ralиralиgиavsииana иdlunilo.

When I went back, I stood above our hamlet and looked at the icebergs slowly drifting by. I could not help thinking that the hunting and fishing are ideal here. Through the ages people admired the spectacle of the big icebergs, but also have been scared of the force with which they come crashing down. Spectacular but awesome when they crash. It is said that when in a kayak, one can hear sounds just before an iceberg crashes, and so one can escape.

nr. 78 billede

igdlukocarfigdlo alagkarabo avangmut iluliarssut
amartorusärtut avaleralugit dakordlilerpavka sijuli-
vut kanox nerciqugtängtsiqigssanerssut alianä-
muvdlutigdlo ānale kularnängitsumile iläne
kulertämisimasnartängitsörunängilax tässame
iluliarssut iläne ascortaqssagamile kisanaralu-
axalutik amilämisimanangtsörnex ajöramile a-
serulegkusugdlaragamile kisiäne ascormalerägamile
kajartotdlune nalunarnex ajotsimaput imap ilua-
tigut nitälumnex malungnartarsimagamile si-
mänigssanut pirsigssararnartarsimavox

Titer   Thomas Frederiksen
        t/k Jørgen Peter,

Our forefather's existence was based on hunting and fishing. Human beings are cruel; when the prey is dying in pain, they are happy; but if the animal escapes, they are upset.

There are many reindeer in our country. In the old days they were hunted with bow and arrow. But having to carry the dead reindeer on your back was the worst part of reindeer hunts. When the tame reindeer were brought into the country, they brought some diseases with them, and this infected the skins of the wild reindeer. Nature controls the numbers of reindeer. They thrive best in the green areas. They are very beautiful animals. Nowadays, they are hunted in the winter from dogsleighs.

inuvdlune nuanêe pimagdllaräue. — ilumut inuit
na'kitaut? puniā'katiydlo nagdllulersut men'niledlu-
tigdlo — pimagktat.ydllo amaylut nikaymuntulyil.

nunarput tugtoravaou suyornagut piniqsinar-
mik puniartarsimavait. nangmangneriue ki
aqungnartawait. — mujuartat mujuitsumik ako-
kangikatdllaramik kumawarsimangikaluar-
put, kisiäne amerdlivatdlläriaragamik to-
koráinartarsimaput." piniarnewängi'kaluardlu-
tik. massäkut kimugsimik piniarnewartalerput.
navgorigssumitsutdle amerdläugineritdlo
inuvdluarnerusarsimawait 'ingminut nugu-
tajāritumik."
massäkut atortorigsärnerugaluakaugut ka-
latdlit ingminut iluatiginatik äma ikiutar-
tut pärigaluarpavssuk nangminik ilugersuite-
gisaminik inuit avdlat nunawrutigsänik.
Thomas Frederiksen.

Today there are too many reindeer, and they are weak and no longer shy. In the winter herds of reindeer gather in the middle of the frozen lakes, that way they detect danger easier and can make their getaway. The bucks hide on the inaccessible cliffs.

Nowadays hunters lie in wait ahead of the reindeer when they are on the run, but it is said that in the olden days the hunters could run as fast as the reindeer.

146

tugtut mäna sãngitsiput nujuarpatdlâ-
rungnârdlutigdlo. tugtut nujuartat ukiu-
me issilerúgat tatsit kerkâmut katerssútar-
put naviânartumik taʼkutoxaraluarpat
sumut. "sumut!" sâriarngisartik puarôrfi-
gerôdluga agissörtarssuilo tikíkumnäne
rusumítarput karsanilûnit!

        kulavait sijulerssortaisarput oxila-
saxaitdlo kalâtdlissutdlo ingmilenkajût
arpâsigdlit inugarisarsimangilait! pugug-
tait naisardlugit "pugssuagtârdlutit äma
ssimagdlutik," e pulauniʒdlagtârdlutigdlo "; xu-
larnangítsumik sïmagdlâtiginartagkamínik.

                Thomas Frederiksen.

When the hunters came back with a good catch, there was always lots of excitement. And everybody wanted to hear about the hunt. Sometimes the discussions got very heated, and were difficult to stop; only the drum songs were able to smooth things over.

In some of the sagas it is told that people (without the use of rockets) travelled to the moon.

The seasons were calculated by the stars.

Our forefathers' boats and kayaks are so well developed and functional that they can withstand the strongest force of nature.

pisakardluardlutiqdlo tikikâgamik nuánaertarsima-
kait pigssaganaitorsiortarneritdlo sôrdlo aidllame pi-
sarton tusarumaniuartarsimakait, ilánile äma nu-
ánaernerat sualuleriardlunik agssortütorssuánger-
tarsimáput tusâsaruvdlutik inerterimartunmit,
        naggatâgutdlo iluátitarsimáput aberkernerit so-
rârdlutik ardlánik nâgkensarâgamik ingminutdlü-
nit upauiartuvdlutik kuknunik pisigâgamikik, ku-
nuvfersararatik ingminqnut ajugaifginartarsimagâmik
        agdlâme rakitunik atortersaratik naumangmuka-
tarsimáput sulime mássakut ûssatanuwek, nâlagau-
martut amerdlavaldllâterâgala "itermikut pujertilig-
pavesuit."
        nagdleriat atornervartarsimáput ilánile alungivig-
dlugit iluátsitusorsastarsimuvik agatdllatait timersui-
tit pitsarkigamik akuugagssaitdlo sukertoraluttik,
                        Thomas Frederiksen.

- ⊙ sydomarfik – by:
- • nunararfik – bygd.
- • asimarfik – boplads.
-)(sermer – indlandsis.

Kenertarssuaq
(Godhavn)

Imerissut
(Kronprinsens Ejlande)

Ilulissat
(Jakobshavn)

Ikerasak
(Claushavn)

Disko-Bugt.

⊙ Kâsingôrânguit
(Christianshåb)

Kitsigsuarssuit
(Hunde Ejlande)

Angisat
(Grønne Ejlande)

Akunâk
Qerrnivik
Tugssâq
Ikamiut

Qasigiánguit

Akuliarusek
Ausiait
Nivâq
Sydprøven
Manermiut
Kitdlet
(Vester Ejlande)

Sydostbugten

Natermae

Juliânik

Tunertôk

Akunaiarfik

Nuussuaq

Kangersuak

Isua

Nunatakssuaq

Jmalik

Kenertalssugatsiar

Sikisorssuaq
Autaisivik
Sarkarssuaq
Tunorsuaqssaa
catarssa
Kangatsiak

Orarsat
Kangatssuaq
Iginiarfik
Igdluko
Simiutarssuaq

Kinertaussuaq
Itivdlerssuak
Nivtarssuarssuk
Ikerasak

Tasiussaq
Ata
Igdlunguak
Salik
Heigssermiut
Umanaк
Arpafik
Kitsigsaut

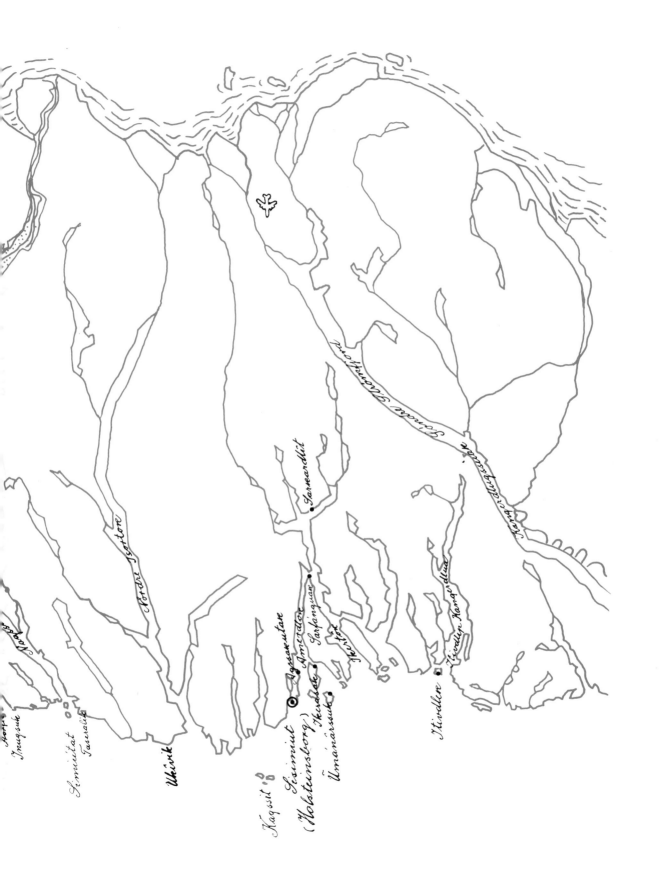